Prison Wisdom

Writing with Inmates

Katya Sabaroff Taylor

Katya Taylor

Published by EWH Press
Ormond Beach, FL 32176

www.ewhpress.com

EWH Press first printing, March 2017

Cover art by Frank Walls
Cover and book design by Bryan Mitchell & Katya Sabaroff Taylor
Edited by Jeff Stoner

Printed in the United States of America

ISBN 978-0-9903500-9-5

FLORIDA, 2017

Dedication

To Robert Kingston
and our chance meeting
on the streets of New York City
more than 50 years ago

TABLE OF CONTENTS

SECTION I

Section II

I knew by the age of 14 that I was a writer (I wrote my first "serious" poem at age 11). But it wasn't until my 30s—four decades ago—that I began offering writing in the community. My impetus was to share the benefits of the writing life with others. At first I called my classes "Keeping a Creative Journal." The title later morphed into "Writing Our Life Stories," or simply "LifeStories," a blend of prose and poetry, fact and fancy. In my 40s, I added haiku poetry to the mix. I had been enchanted with this ancient Japanese "essence poem" since I was first introduced to it in college.

I believed wholeheartedly from the start, and I still believe, that writing in a group is transformative, that we all have wisdom to share, and that everyone has a writer hidden within "waiting for expression."

I have written not only with prisoners but also with school children, the elderly, the dying, with artists and social workers. I have written with self-help groups, in churches and YMCAs, in healing centers, hospital outreach programs, in college classrooms, and around my dining room table. My methodology (how I evoke stories and poems from my students, no matter their age, education, or lifestyle) has evolved, but in a sense has remained constant:

One: Participants sit in a circle or around an oblong table so we can all see one another.

Two: Prompts or "seed phrases" are given, and we all write on the same topics (i.e. *I remember a room, A lonely time, Once I believed, Saying goodbye...*).

Three: It is safe to share. Students are told, "No one can write your story but you"; there is no competition, no critiquing, no good writers and bad writers—just people letting the muse guide their pen.

Four: When we share, all listen with full attention, and everyone participates.

Lastly: I write with my students. I am no better or worse, more talented or creative, than they are. I am as vulnerable and as brave in sharing my life experiences, hurts and joys.

I believe that my success in eliciting writing from people from all walks of life has been made possible by my unconditional regard for each student, my sincere attention when they read, my affirmation of their value as a human being. Without this, the exercises and prompts would lose their power. Without this, there would be no alchemy.

An intimacy is born that goes beyond much of what passes for connection in the modern world. The differences between us—age, class, skin color, manner of dress, level of education—disappear as our stories unfold. This may sound impossible or at least unlikely, but it is true. Here is the testimony of one inmate at the end of our sessions together:

This writing class has brought a bunch of men from many different races and religions together. Inside these walls we must all be on alert at all times from one another, but in this small writing class we are all together as one, as we express our feelings and emotions in this journal. It's funny how a small class like this could bring a bunch of men together to make them better human beings.

Richard, FCI, Tallahassee

In the last two decades, I have entered a variety of prisons and written with hundreds of men and women, preparing twelve anthologies that I now have in my hands as a source, a testimony, of these individuals' lives, stories, poems, hopes, fears—a testimony of a fraction of the humanity "out of sight and mind." (The title of one of our digests.)

It is to honor these men and women, to hold up the mirror so we can all see—not only them, but ourselves in the glass—that I compile this book. In reading *Prison Wisdom*, as one friend suggested, we will not say, "There but for the grace of God go I," but "There I am."

I invite all who visit these pages to pick up a pen and write. You may not be behind bars, but if you do not tell your stories, when you die "a library will burn." Your life matters, your words matter. I hope this becomes abundantly clear as you read on....

Katya Sabaroff Taylor
Spring 2016

Prologue: On Writing in Prison

Friends have often asked me how I first became interested in teaching creative writing in the prisons. The story begins a long time ago. I was only eighteen and playing hooky from my summer job as a nurse's aide one sunny morning when I met a man begging on the streets of New York City. Because there was something I could trust about his face, I invited him to my third-floor brownstone walk-up, gave him lunch, and we spent the day talking about our lives. He was an unemployed construction worker, I an aspiring poet.

Some weeks later, when I went to visit him, I discovered that he was in jail. His ex-wife was dead and he was being blamed for it. We began to write to one another, becoming confidantes, chronicling our deepest thoughts, feelings, and dreams. While serving his time, he started including pencil drawings in his letters. Impressed with his natural talent, I encouraged him, and he did go on to become a skilled painter. Although Kingston is dead now, we did reunite upon his release, and we continued to write to one another, sharing our lives for more than 25 years. It was he who showed me once and for all that a prisoner has a soul, a life, a dream, and is cut of the same vulnerable and complex fabric as myself. This lesson, this truth, has only become more pronounced, more true, as the years go by.

After earning my master's in education and working as a journalist, supporting various causes in the 70s and 80s, I married and had a child. (It was shortly after my daughter Alana was born that Kingston died, before he could paint her portrait.) In 1990 my family settled in Tallahassee, Florida. Once my young daughter was in school, I opened myself to a professional re-emergence, and in my seeking I met B., who taught GED classes at the local county jail.

"Oh," I smiled eagerly, "I've always wanted to offer writing in the prisons!"

"Well, why don't you?" he said.

And so I began volunteering once a week, passing through gates and beneath barbwire fences into a doublewide trailer, through whose windows you could actually see a few trees, birds and the open sky. It was here I met dozens of men and women (in segregated groups), all awaiting trial, all dressed in their plain brown or blue prison garb, all hungry for substance, for liberation, for expressing what lay pent up within. We wrote together and read our words aloud, unmasking ourselves in the process.

Later on I taught in federal prisons, with both male and female populations. While writing, the bars momentarily seem to disappear. And, as I tell my classes, "We are all equal under the law of the pen." I've discovered, and my students have discovered, again and again, that we all have something to live for and to share, we all have that common and unique spark waiting to be ignited. We all have pens in our hands and we all write.

I often wonder about the act of fate that led me to invite a hungry man to share a meal. I dedicate *Prison Wisdom* to my friend and mentor, Robert Kingston. Without you, this book would never have been.

SECTION I: ANTHOLOGIES OF INMATE WRITING

The power of the mind through the pen brings

Freedom!

Graphic by Billi-Jo, FCI

Introduction

I first began offering "Creative Journaling" (forerunner to "LifeStories"), in 1982 for an extended education course at a local college. As the sessions continued, it occurred to me that the writing deserved to be "saved," in a one-of-a-kind edition, to share with all the members of the class. Thus, the idea for my first literary digest, or writing anthology, was born.

The students are asked to choose their favorite pieces and turn in a camera-ready copy that I would then take to a print shop. I created a cover and table of contents to finish the collection. For the final class, we all collated the pages, punched them with a paper punch and bound them with several strands of embroidery thread. I continued to gather my students' work into anthology form from then on.

When I offered my first inmate writing class in Tallahassee's Leon County Jail, in 1991, it made perfect sense to do for my students what I had done for all the others who had come before. Again, I asked each person to choose their favorite writing pieces (to make a star by each entry in their writing journals), and I rented a large electric typewriter—yes, this was before the personal computer revolution—and typed up their entries. In the case of the county jail, there was also a variety of art that had been produced in the GED class that I cut and pasted into the document. I then gave the thick manuscript to the jail print shop to reproduce (with a cover created by an inmate artist).

Each student was given two copies: one for themselves, and one to send home to family or friends. (In many cases, later on, these anthologies were also put into the prison's library so many inmates could access them.)

I made up my mind to continue the tradition in every prison class I taught. I saw what it meant to the inmates to see their writings published, to hold the anthology in their hands and read aloud their words that were now, in a sense, "immortal." For most of my prison students, this would be the first time their writing was valued, the first time they saw themselves as "writers." Being a longtime writer, it was a very moving experience for me to see their joy—this is not too strong a word—in seeing their words in print.

In the earliest prison anthologies, I organized the material by "seed phrase" (e.g. *"At this very moment,"* or *"I remember a room"*). In this way I hoped to show the reader how different individuals responded to the same prompt—how each student is a unique individual with their own story, their own way of seeing and experiencing life. In some cases I separated the poems from the prose, and put guided visualizations and other "fictions" into their own pages, in part to educate the reader in how many ways writing can be evoked and creativity summoned.

In later anthologies, I began to group the writings by individual, to showcase a variety of their writings in one place, rather than scattered throughout by genre or seed prompt.

When I began putting together *Prison Wisdom*, I struggled over how best to present a huge volume of material. Should I put all the haiku poetry produced from 1991 to 2015, in one section, for example, regardless of which prison it came from? Should I put all the guided visualizations together? After much wrestling with this question, I decided it made more sense to organize the writing chronologically by each anthology in turn, starting with Leon County Jail in 1991, all the way up to FCI, Tallahassee, in 2015. In that way, every class would have its own integrity, its own unique literary expression.

I presented each anthology by highlighting the cover, as if to invite the reader to now enter the realm of this particular group of writers. It was satisfying to ask students to create the cover graphic, which in most cases, came to pass. (In some classes, no artist stepped forward, so I put together the cover image.)

Students signed up for my LifeStories classes of their own free will—they were not mandated to take the course. In the beginning I volunteered in a GED class, offering the writing as an "extra" to their studying to pass the test. In later non-GED classes, students signed up after flyers were put up in the units. I kept the number of students to no larger than twelve, so that there would be time to both write and share in a limited amount of time (most classes were either 90 minutes or two hours).

To further "humanize" the inmates, I received permission to call my students by their first names (typically prisoners are addressed by their last names), and they were allowed to call me "Katya," rather than "Mrs. Taylor." This may seem like a small thing, but it created an intimacy that encouraged each of us to write—and share—from the heart.

Word of mouth among inmates meant that I had no trouble filling the classes, usually taught in Spring and Fall; and one time, to accommodate those who were still at FCI, I offered a "graduate" workshop, when students from different LifeStories classes gathered together in a new configuration.

I think it is important to share here that the words you are about to read, most of which were written in five- to seven-minute segments, have not been edited by me, but were written just as you read them. I did occasionally correct a spelling error, which I have done in many cases before I ever began teaching in the prisons. While writing in a group, under a time limitation, there is a creative energy that permits and encourages a flow of expression. When students are told: "There is no wrong way to write," and "No one can tell your story but you," the inner critic that holds many of us back from creation loses its power.

I have attempted to show student writings complete on the page, rather than spilling the text over to the next. In a sense, then, each page is a complete manuscript. In a few instances this was not possible, but in general, this is how I present the material. My hope is that you, the reader, will not race through this "encyclopedia of humanity," but pause after each entry. Allow yourself to experience fully the substance and emotion of each story and poem. What does this person have to offer you? How would you have responded to this assignment?

I welcome you now to the writings of one hundred and fifteen individuals, whose penned words are offered here—no longer "out of sight and mind," but in the present moment sharing their words of wisdom, sorrow, and happiness.

Katya Sabaroff Taylor

Cover art by Robert

Leon County Jail: *Hey You!*, 1991–1992

It was in the fall of 1991 that I began my initial foray writing with inmates at the local county jail, volunteering to come in once a week to their GED class. Jail, as opposed to prison, is where inmates who cannot make bail are waiting for sentencing. This wait can go on for months, as I discovered, giving me a lot of time to write with the same individuals. (I appreciated the continuity, while lamenting a system that kept people locked up in limbo for such long stretches of time.) Men and women were segregated in separate classes; the men wrote with men, the women with women. Little did I know when I entered that doublewide trailer for the first time what creativity would flow, but I was about to find out.

The writings that follow are excerpted from the two inmate anthologies entitled "Hey You!" As always, I begin the very first class with the seed phrase "At this very moment," and to set the scene, I am including my first piece ever written with inmates (also included in the anthology). Each writing assignment is usually from five to seven minutes long. We share before moving on to the next prompt. Although men and women wrote separately, I have combined them in this account.

NOTE: Although inmates used their full names for all anthologies, when getting ready to publish Prison Wisdom *we felt that, to protect the privacy of the writers, we would only use first names. We know the writers will recognize themselves when they hold a copy of this book in their hands.*

At This Very Moment

At this very moment I am sitting in a warm (over-heated) rₒ
men at the Leon County jail, fulfilling a promise of years agₒ
friend Kingston was in prison and our letters were a journal that ₁
years – while he served his time – and longer after his release, mₐ
lifetime. Because of the extreme cold, unseasonal in Tallahassee, Floₗ
there are only a few students here, but "when two or more gather" in tₗ
name of something, a powerful force is released to radiate inward and
outward.

At this very moment the blue-black ink is like arterial blood or like the
depths of a fathomless ocean, royal and enduring. My little mortality
swells with hope. Perhaps this life means something. Perhaps all I think
and do and feel is worth something too. At this very moment the coffee
is hot and bitter and my tongue loosened…*

*At that time, instructors had access to coffee while teaching -- I brought in
the cream.

Katya

At this very moment, a moment of solitude, peaceful and tranquil, a
feel for freedom of the spirit, to reach up and out and to soar above and
beyond, to see and feel the fresh crispness of the morning air and to smell
the sweetness of Springtime. The bright flowers in full bloom, the birds
singing a joyful tune, the butterflies floating so peacefully above and
beyond, and the animals dancing, full of joy and charm. Winter's chill
has passed us by.

Keir

At This Very Moment

At this very moment, I see this imaginary alignment of rusty metal bars, is this real or fantasy? I look at the yellow chipped paint on the walls, am I here or is it just an illusion in my mind? I look at this stained window. My mind is playing tricks on me.

I can't even remember what a tree looks like. Am I here or am I gone? Do I know right from wrong? I see the same faces through this wall. This all must be an illusion in my mind. All this must be my mind playing tricks on me.

Mike

Graphic by Robert

When I Look In The

When I look in the mirror I see a black man ee
to control his destiny.

                                          as half the powe.

When I look in the mirror I see the times when
though they would go very well, the times when I vd not look as
didn't care.
                                          ger and just

when I look in the mirror I see all of the things a little po.
can bring, the love, the hate, yet all of this is just a part of red green
I look in the mirror I see all of these parts in me.   When

                                          Loren

This morning. How deep did you look when you looked in that mirror?

                                          Mr. K

Looking back over those tender but wasted years, I could have made a
difference in someone's life and also in my own life. I could have built
more but instead I wasted more. I could have loved more but instead I
hated more. Time, time, time, what have you done to me?

                                          Kenneth

I close my eyes, and what do I see?
Green fields and blue skies...
I open my eyes and what do I see?
Four blank walls staring back at me.

                                          Melissa

write about the seasons and changing weather.
In my classe... ritten about a rainy day.
Here are tv...

A Rainy Day

I was as... write for five minutes about a rainy day. At first I wanted
to writ... what it was like to grow up in a tin top house on rainy
days, ... ow the rains pounded at whatever emotions happened to be
on th... face at the time.

Th... was called into the next room and given some bad news. Rain fell
fr... my eyes and all the things I felt flooded my heart. It was indeed a
rainy day.

Defonza

When it's a rainy day, I feel as if I have no worries in the world. I feel
my self drawn into all the romantic aspects of life, like sitting in front
of a fireplace with a big warm fire burning brightly, holding hands and
snuggled real close to the one I love. Drinking wine and feeling love for
each other where words are not needed. The rain is falling against the
roof saying "All your worries are over. You are safe now."

Gail

And, on sunshine:

Sunlight

As I write, a sunbeam stretches across
my paper, and gives me the incentive
to go on.

Twanna

When I Look In The Mirror I See

When I look in the mirror I see a black man, one who has half the power to control his destiny.

When I look in the mirror I see the times when things did not look as though they would go very well, the times when I was younger and just didn't care.

when I look in the mirror I see all of the things a little power and green can bring, the love, the hate, yet all of this is just a part of reality. When I look in the mirror I see all of these parts in me.

Lorenzo

This morning. How deep did you look when you looked in that mirror?

Mr. K

Looking back over those tender but wasted years, I could have made a difference in someone's life and also in my own life. I could have built more but instead I wasted more. I could have loved more but instead I hated more. Time, time, time, what have you done to me?

Kenneth

I close my eyes, and what do I see?
Green fields and blue skies...
I open my eyes and what do I see?
Four blank walls staring back at me.

Melissa

A Rainy Day

I was asked to write for five minutes about a rainy day. At first I wanted to write about what it was like to grow up in a tin top house on rainy days, and how the rains pounded at whatever emotions happened to be on the surface at the time.

Then I was called into the next room and given some bad news. Rain fell from my eyes and all the things I felt flooded my heart. It was indeed a rainy day.

Defonza

When it's a rainy day, I feel as if I have no worries in the world. I feel my self drawn into all the romantic aspects of life, like sitting in front of a fireplace with a big warm fire burning brightly, holding hands and snuggled real close to the one I love. Drinking wine and feeling love for each other where words are not needed. The rain is falling against the roof saying "All your worries are over. You are safe now."

Gail

Sunlight

As I write, a sunbeam stretches across
my paper, and gives me the incentive
to go on.

Twanna

My Dream

One night I dreamed that I was a king in a castle. All the knights were around the round table to get ready to fight other Kingdoms, like fighting for Freedom. So they fought and fought to be free, to be free.

Brent

My Dream

One recurring dream I often have is of sitting under a palm tree, as if I were in a trance. All of a sudden I wake up. It is very hot. I start walking down a dirt road. I look up and see a flock of seagulls. I continue to watch them until I trip over some driftwood. That's when I see the ocean. I think about how hot it is, so I run across the beach until I reach the end and plunged into the water...

Tawanna

I Have A Dream

I have a dream of pain come to past. I live in a world where there is no controlling, people love freely and hate is not known. Nature is our friend and we respect it. No more storms, just tranquility. We live with an open mind and heart. Innocence is our nature.

Chris

I Remember

I remember sunlight on the bay, the warmth of the world. And those caring giants, ever present, as I crawled through the morning of my life.

I remember winter nights, crystal cold warmth, fire in my heart, and my first taste of manhood before the glowing stone fireplace. It was then the midday of my life.

I remember bright spring, the returning freshness of the world, the need to love, the happiness of eternal sharing, and the making of life.

And now I see sunlight on the bay, and feel the warmth of the world. And I am the ever-present giant, loving and helping my daughter through the morning of her life.

Anthony

Graphic by Randy

I Remember

I remember beautiful things behind bars. There's all those times we fed the seagull. It's funny, after that first time they reappeared at every meal. They became our friends.

There's the night the Dorm was filled with silence... Every eye was watching, every ear was listening, and every mind deep in thought as we sat quietly and watched a Christmas special. I took a moment to look around. I saw a beautiful thing...every face smiling, tears of joy streaming down my friends' faces.

All the tears that fall behind these bars are not of joy, but fear and pain from broken hearts. Yet there is still beauty. To see a friend sitting with the upset one holding her hand and lending her shoulder, only to give some comfort behind these cold steel bars.

Then there's those small purple flowers growing in between the cracks in our paved yard. We leave them growing, so everyone can enjoy the beautiful flowers.

I'll never forget the hours we spend dancing on the picnic table, making our own music, having a good time behind these bars.

You can see beautiful things too, but you have to look, and not with your eyes. You look through your heart.

Just look into the mirror, and you will see the most beautiful thing of all – You!

Kandi

A Childhood Turning Point

I had a dog named Blackie, he was part collie. I had him ever since I was three years old and he was very close to me. My parents were never around—my dad in the service and my mom was a nurse on call, twenty four hours a day. The dog became my best and only friend. We shared my bed and shared the same food at dinner. He lived until I was twelve years old. After he died, a serious change came over me. I became very withdrawn for a long time. I couldn't understand why my only friend had gone away and left without me.

Homer

Saying Goodbye

It's possible, of course, that saying goodbye wasn't what I wanted to say to Vinnie.

Certainly, it had to have been that "goodbye" was the last of all things I wanted to say; stay alive, stay awake, don't leave me here to bear the pain, it's all my fault. I should have stopped you, I should have told your mother…

The bleeding wouldn't stop. I couldn't get you to keep your eyes open. I could only hold you and cry, and listen for any words you might try to say.

Were you saying goodbye?

Robert

A Mythological Person

I was fortunate enough to live with my grandfolks when I was a mere child. My grandmother was half authentic gypsy and half American Indian. She had the eyes of a mystic. She spoke more often with them than her mouth. She read palms, had a crystal ball, and raised goats, to the despair of the rest of the family.

She comes to me in happiness through the medium of rain and wind, which she loves. Her smell was green and new – wise in the ways of man and the world, and never surprised over progress, as she expected and anticipated changes.

Katie

My Mother's Photograph

Since I could remember I never knew my mother. She passed away when I was two.

One day I was going through some boxes in the attic, dusty, dirty. I overturned a small wooden chest. Inside was a photograph of a beautiful woman sitting on a classic car wearing a blood red dress, the kind of dress with low cleavage, and wearing bright red shoes to match.

I wondered to myself, who could this be?

I asked my Dad. He told me: "This is a picture of your mother the day I proposed."

Anonymous

The Death Of My Mother

I have to begin from the beginning and repeat: she's dead. As if it's just struck me. And I find myself drowning, engulfed by the disorder of the current, wanting to seize her hand to bring me to shore.

Some days I can look at her photograph and the image revives me, reinforces her for me. On other days, I gaze at her and am blinded by tears. Newly bereft.

This outpouring of feeling… I'm crying on Mom's shoulder. I'm wailing into the wind, sobs against a crashing surf. You come, and you go. I had her once, and now she's gone.

Sandra

My Child

Boy or girl, Adam or Ashley, will be beautiful. If it's a boy I hope he's rough and rugged but also clever and courteous. If it's a girl I hope she's soft and delicate but not naïve. I want my children to be determined, yet open minded. I want them to be smart but also let them have common sense. Even if they have none of these, they'll still have my love.

Jason

When I Think Of Peace

I'm sitting here thinking about what is peace. For me, I'm looking for what is called Inner Peace. It comes when a person can give unconditional love to everyone and everything. Some people think peace is like the calm water of the ocean, never realizing all death and confusion going on under the surface, or like getting off a merry go round with loud music when everything stops. But remember you must regain your balance to walk away.

Now I must ask the world: "How do you find Inner Peace?"

Wade

When I Think Of Death

What will happen when I die? Will I feel my flesh rot and decay or will I go to a place in the sky where I will feel peace in me? Or will I go down far underground where fear and pain fills your soul? Or will it be like turning off a light that disappears into the dark of the night?

Mike

Nothing

Lying in the dark I hear nothing.
What is Nothing?
I say it is the sound the air creates
when you're lonely.

Tawanna

My Magical Object

It's black with two pockets on the outside and one on the inside. It is a genuine hooded leather jacket, given to me when my father passed away. This was his jacket that he used to wear out on the town. It still carries his presence inside of it.

My leather jacket gives me a warm feeling, which makes me think he's still here on earth. It makes me think back to those wonderful summer days of being home in Chicago eating gyros with dad, and watching movies. It also brings back memories of going fishing, and his "You're my baby," lectures. All of these make my jacket more than special, they make it magical.

Olivia

A Precious Object

My father had a Rolex since the time I became aware. Before Rolex was a big deal. $125.00 and a couple of beers my father got that Rolex in Germany. In the Navy, too young for World War II but before Vietnam, he had that watch that he always wears. I've never seen it off his wrist. I don't believe it has ever broken or gone into the shop. But one time I swear I saw it stop. The only time, maybe a figment of my imagination, a cobweb in my mind. To this day I'm not sure. For when the life flowed back into him, I know I heard its reassuring tick, tick.

Marie

A Powerful Moment

My most powerful moment was the first time I ever looked into the eyes of the man I love. Every time I feel the power of his love throughout my whole body. The power gets stronger each and every time my eyes meet his.

I need that look right now.

Kasey

My Most Powerful Moment

My most powerful moment started at 3 o'clock in the morning. I was in labor with my first child. The pain hurt so much I said "Stop! The time is here, so just do it and get it over with."

So, at 5:08 in the morning, I birthed an eight pound baby boy. That was the most powerful moment. The power that I didn't know I really had.

Delina

Drawing by T.A.

The Essence Exercise is a "poetic" way to describe who we are in metaphorical terms. It is fascinating to see how different individuals respond to the same prompt.

The Essence Exercise

If I were an animal, I'd be a bird, an eagle because eagles are one and few, living in a world unknown to me, flying free, ruling, acting, as kings in the sky.

If I were a musical instrument, I'd be the baton that leads the orchestra to every perfect note.

If I were a piece of furniture, I would be the Lazy Chair that puts anyone to sleep. To be able to relax people.

If I were an article of clothing, I know I'd never be the sweater that hangs in the closet lonely, waiting for a cool day.

If I were a color in the rainbow, I'd be yellow like gold, to be as shiny as the sun, just to be noticed by everyone. To blind them with beauty…

Kandi

If I were an animal, I would be unchanged and wild, nocturnal in life, shy of the light. A Florida panther, an abyss in the night.

If I were a musical instrument, a Charvel would be my choice. Full of power and endless chords.

If I were a piece of furniture, I have no choice. Just waiting for someone to use you sounds rather boring.

If I were a color, I would be something always looked at but seldom seen. The colors of the sky in the day or the night…

Yale

The Essence Exercise

If I were an animal, I'd be a peacock, for obvious reasons.

If I were a musical instrument, I would be a bassoon or trombone, because they are long and thin in character, with a mellow sound. The trombone with flashes of brassiness, both with a wide range.

If I were a piece of furniture, I would be a file cabinet. A storehouse of information, anything you want, it's there for the searching.

If I were a color I would be is the color that I am. Brown. With its beauty it has a wide spectrum and many shades.

If I were an article of clothing, I would be a hat. It is always at the top and always seen.

Robert

If I were an animal, I'd be a lion because I was born under that Zodiac sign.

If I were a musical instrument, I'd be a drum because the drum carries rhythm, cadence and control.

If I were a piece of furniture, I'd be a rocking chair, because I like relaxing, deep thought

If I were a piece of clothing, I'd be a coat without seams, I would be one of a kind.

If I were a color, I'd be black, because I could find all the other colors inside.

Defonza

To engage my students' imaginations, I lead them on a "Guided Visualization." Below are two different journeys. In the first, the students are led to a sunny beach, and while walking along the shore they see a bottle wash up. They are asked to pick up the bottle and read the message inside. In the second, students are guided through a meadow, and up a hill, until they see a cabin. On the porch are two rocking chairs, one for them and one for "a wise being." They ask the wise one a question, and then they are given a gift to take back with them.

Message In A Bottle

I'm walking on a beach of white sands, width of twenty feet, length is round and out of eyesight. The sky is blue with little cotton puff clouds. The forest is green and thick with trees and bushes. I feel content with being here on the beach, just walking, enjoying my walk, not worrying about the future. I see and pick up the bottle with curiosity:

"You are precious!!"

Chris

As I was walking along the beach, I felt so free, so good-looking. The warm sand on my feet, looking at the waves come over my feet, was the nicest feeling of peace. I looked down and what did I see, a bottle with a note inside for me. I read the words from long ago from the man I loved back then. I took the words he once more wrote for me, put them in my pocket and walked along, so carefree.

Patty

As I walked aimlessly along the Gulf I found a bottle floating in the surf, and as I uncorked and retrieved the single piece of brown rapper paper, there was one single word. Simply: HELP!

Greg

Cabin Porch Visualization

As I approached the cabin porch with the two rocking chairs, there sat my ex-boyfriend from Georgia. We've always said to each other that we wanted to get old together and rock side by side in two rocking chairs. So as I sat there in silence, I've always wondered did he really love and care for me as much as I did for him?

Then when he answered me and told me Yes, and that he always would make me happy, it made me want to cry, especially when he reached in his bag and gave me a friendship ring that I knew would last forever.

But I was very very sad when I had to turn away and leave him, it made my heart sink. As I walked back through the meadow and looked up at the sky I knew it was a night I would never forget...

Sharon

The meadow was so green, so lush, I had to take off my shoes. In the rocking chair was an older version of myself – long white braids, a white muslin robe tied with a silk sash.

"What can I do to make my life more meaningful, less fragmented, less tense?" I asked.

She smiled. "Never hurry," was her answer.

Then, she gave me a jar of golden honey to remember the sweetness of my life.

Katya

Cabin Porch Haiku

As we were sitting
our talk became fulfilling
our hearts were with joy

Kathleen

POETRY

In class we experiment with various forms of poetry. Sometimes it is a takeoff on a famous poet, like Walt Whitman, who sometimes starts his long phrase "list poems" with "I have seen"; or William Carlos Williams, who wrote brief poems in two phrase stanzas beginning with "I have seen" or "So much depends upon..." We learn the structure of haiku poems, as well as create free verse poems and "hyperbole" I AM poems (exaggerating our human qualities). You will see all of these in the following pages.

Takeoff On Walt Whitman

I Have Seen

I have seen too much, too little, not enough
Sometimes I look around and wonder
Is this the end or when will it ever begin?
Looking out of these eyes
Are they really mine?
Trying to capture the version of looking
From the inside to the outside
With these eyes.
Stop, what have I seen?
I guess I've seen life.

Kenneth

I have seen this place before.
Surely I have been here many a time.
Not just in my deepest of thought, but in person.
Maybe not tangible, but yes, there have I been.
Looking far far out over the universe,
No time, no space, no one place, no two places,
Just out in the beyond.
I look and look, no certain destination,
No imaginary lines...

Tony

I Have Seen

I have seen many wonderful things
and things not so wonderful
I have seen life's beginning and life's ending
I have seen the look of happiness
and the look of anger
I have seen pain through the faces of many
and through the face of a baby, joy
I have seen the reaching out of one
while a whole world withdraws.
I have seen understanding, confusion,
wisdom and ignorance all in the same.

Charles

I have seen the lights go out
the lights go on
I have seen dark clouds mass
and slender sunbeams stroke Spring trees
I have seen people laugh and scream
and curse and sigh
I myself have laughed and screamed,
cursed and cried.
I have seen animals proud and free
in the wilds, pausing to sniff the scented air,
and animals caged and sorrowful
pacing the tiny concrete slab.
I have seen rainbows over sandstone cliffs
and lightning rip ferocious skies.
I have seen tenderness in men and violence
and in women the same...
I have seen lights flicker but not go out
I have seen what goes on and can never
be taken away
what goes on and breathes
what goes on and sings
what poetry is made of
what our hearts say is true.

Katya

Takeoff On William Carlos Williams

I Have Seen

Sunrise come
as usual

glowing, red, powerful
and new

giving of itself
again

see you tomorrow
old friend

Defonza

So Much Depends

So much depends
on keeping close

But yet we are
kept so far away

I question the logic
of the leaders and followers

I often wonder
what is to happen day by day

I dislike certain lessons, but
there's education in many rooms here

Dwayne

I AM

I am a kernel put into the ground
I am that same kernel peeping out over the land
I am the child just left its mother's womb.
I am the ocean on a hot summer's day.
I am the lull that comes before the storm.
I am the fire that burns away the forest.
I am the volcano that erupts so viciously.
I am the bomb that destroys anything around it.
I am the sun when it goes down in the West.
I am Spring when everything starts to bloom.

Louis

I AM

I am the thunderbolt at the top of the mountain
I am the tune you can't stop humming
I am the hope in the locked up heart
I am so much money you could never spend me
I am the oasis deep in the desert
I am the rainbow in the crystal goblet
I am the bread in the starving child's pocket
I am the photo in the golden locket
I am the map of a brave new world
I am a poem continually in the making
I am the slipper that can't stop dancing
I am the whir in the hummingbird's wings
I am more than the sum of all these things.

Katya

I Have Known You

I have known you since birth
and you grow right before my eyes
I feed you
I give you water
Love
Companionship
Trust.
I've got my hands dirty
tilling your soil
pulling weeds from around you.
You've pleased me
with your soft, velvet petals
my budding flower.

Justin

Love Goes And Love Comes

Love goes and love comes. Some times
Love comes in a hurry, mighty fast
But I wish I was a bird so I could fly
I wish I was a worm so I could wiggle
because everything inside me wiggles.
I wish I was an eagle so I could soar in the sky
Then I think some times that I might see God.
My mind is so full of love and happiness
I want to be a little stone for people to walk on
Or they could pick me up and choose me
as a precious stone
and they could have me as their own.

David

The Wall

I fear the light of day
I fear the touch of man
I fear all that is around me
So I built this wall
So no one can touch me.
Maybe, just maybe, I might tear
This wall down,
One day.

Michael

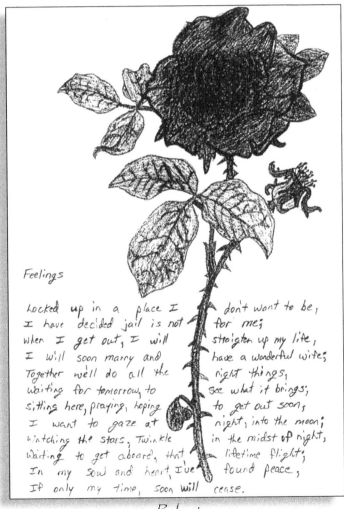

Feelings

Locked up in a place I   don't want to be,
I have decided jail is not   for me;
When I get out, I will   straighten up my life,
I will soon marry and   have a wonderful wife;
Together we'll do all the   right things,
waiting for tomorrow, to   see what it brings;
sitting here, praying, hoping   to get out soon,
I want to gaze at   night, into the moon;
Watching the stars, Twinkle   in the midst of night,
Waiting to get aboard, that   lifetime flight;
In my soul and heart, I've   found peace;
If only my time, soon will   cease.

Robert

HAIKU

Haiku, the ancient Japanese "essence" poem, has only three lines, with a five-seven-five syllable count. In just one image, one moment, a feeling comes alive—one that appears timeless and enduring.

As the night goes by
I sleep a dream that's true
only a brief time

Jose

I am what love is
one who can enter the heart
no scars to the skin

Henrik

My name is Homer
I liked playing against the odds
till death woke me up

Homer

When Spring comes look out
I might just want to go wild
my life's a shambles

Shane

HAIKU

When I think of love
I look at the twinkling stars
saying I'm still here

Justin

I think of things like
coming home, beaches, roses
not war and not death

Lani

Life is like my hair
the colors are woven and deep
every strand lives

Lani

I have no more face
I have become a number
but I can still feel

Barbara

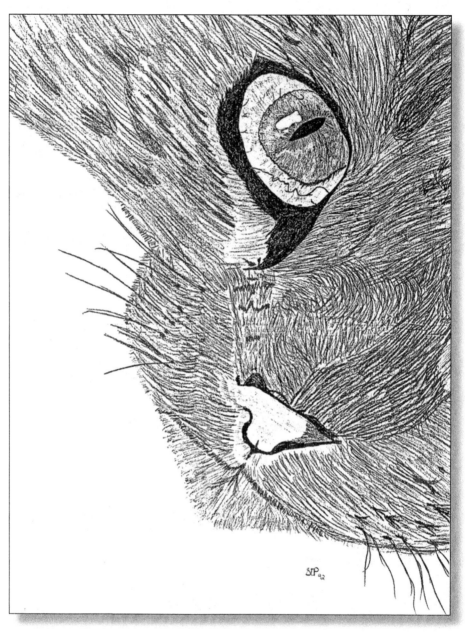

Drawing by Shane

34

OUT OF
SIGHT AND MIND
A WRITER'S JOURNAL

GED CLASS, FCI, TALLAHASSEE

Spring, 1995

Graphic by Skip

FCI Men: *Out Of Sight And Mind,* 1995–1996

After creating two anthologies at Leon County jail, I left to work on other projects. In 1995, I approached the Superintendent of Education at the Federal Correctional Institute (FCI) in Tallahassee, at that time a men's prison, and he warmly welcomed me to offer creative writing in their GED program. Together we created two anthologies, "Out of Sight and Mind," in 1995 and 1996. Excerpts from these compilations follow.

I often introduce the idea of writing in the third person, to give the writer perspective, a way of seeing themselves as a "character" in their own novel of life. In the instances below, Phillip and I both wrote about Today in the Third Person.

Today In The Third Person

Today the hairy man woke up and found out this was not his day. I saw the hairy man go get his breakfast. It looked like he was sleepwalking until he sat down, where he started to eat his cold eggs and hot grits. I saw him walking back to the unit where he made two peanut butter and jelly sandwiches. Then he walked straight to the gate where the man in blue shut the door right in his face, and told him to wait for the next move.

Phillip

Today, the last day of January, reminded her that her birthday month was over. The year 1995 stretched before her like a wide road, bright and clear today, but dim and full of mystery as she tried to look ahead.

Today was her day to teach at FCI, the local prison. She dressed carefully. She wanted to feel comfortable, to look professional but earthy. She wished she could bring in a coffee or teapot and serve everyone homemade breakfast rolls with cinnamon. She pictured the room with a glass ceiling so the blue of the sky could smile down on everyone as they wrote in their journals.

January was slipping quietly away, and February would soon begin. In Florida, February was the month you could put seeds in the ground. She liked that. If you plant a seed, surely something will come up, a flower, a vegetable, a new life.

Katya

My Hands

My hands have done a lot: writing letters to friends and family, working – like washing my car at the car lot. My hands like to play basketball, football, and make love to my girlfriend, hold her hand when we go to the movies on the weekend, take my children to the park to run and play. At night I use my hands to pray for my family and all the people in the world.

Elijah

My hands are creative at times. They can put things together. They can move heavy objects. They can express feelings by caressing every soft woman and holding every small child without hurting them. My hands are very strong but caring.

Cub

A Current Obsession

My current obsession is being surrounded by soft music and a special touch, to only put me at ease. To unlock my mind with a relationship of warmth. My heart pounds fast as I thirst for that urge – like a twink of an eye I've found that space of love.

Juan

Haiku

I love the name Joy
it reminds me of a girl
when I first made love

Barry

Once I Lost

Once I lost my best friend to a world of prison and that best friend happens to be me. Sometimes I wonder will I ever see me again on the outside, looking through my car window? What a feeling that would be! Sometimes I sit and think of so many beautiful things to do and say but there's always this thing called pride and the thought of rejection. I truly believe if I can just find that friend when I first came in I'm sure there will be something to write about.

Eddie

Once I Traveled

Once I traveled on the waters of the Yucatan. The ocean was beautiful and very mysterious. The waters were dark and full of ancient stories. At times I wish I was a part of and could have been there.

Cub

Remembering Back

Remembering back until when I was a little boy. I can still hear the sound of the church piano playing gospel music, only to leave a sense of understanding and praise in my heart. Afterwards we would all gather together in the car or on the back of the truck and have a cookout at the park or on the beach. Then we would retire back home and watch television. Old memories never get washed away.

Juan

I Think Of The Day

I think of the day I go home. How long will it be? How much would the world change? Will I adjust? Will it be like stepping out of a time machine? Man has always feared the unknown. Why should I be any different? Will I be remembered by friends? How about family? How long can family hold on? All we have in here is hope. Hope is like holding on to air. And we all know there is no way to hold on to air.

James

I Can Think Back

I can think back to 1963 when my friends and I used to run in the woods. Those were some refreshing days. The sun was shining bright, the trees were full of life. The birds seemed to have a soft sound of music coming from their wings. Those were the good old days that made me feel so peaceful. My friends have gone to a more peaceful place, and I pray when it's my time, the friends and I can run in that forest, as we did then…

Eddie

Once Upon A Time

Once upon a time a very long time ago I was living in a forest where there was nothing but trees as far as I could see. At times I would go out in the night and I would look up at the sky. The stars were the most beautiful thing you could dream of. I loved living in the forest because there was no noise at all. There were no problems, just peace and quiet.

Sylvester

40

I Remember A Place

I remember a place in Southeast China, in a little town named Kau Loong. I was walking on a path along slippery rocks covered with green moss, and clear water running on top of many different sized pebbles. I could smell the freshness of nature surrounding me. There were many fishes of different colors swimming around.

It was foggy and cool, and birds were singing. Lots of noise ahead of me sounded like heavy rain as I approached. I tried to walk faster to satisfy my curiosity. I finally reached the place that created that noise. What I saw was a big open space. My thoughts were boring and muddy, but what I discovered was the most beautiful place I'd ever seen in my life. It was really worth my adventure.

I saw a very tall and massive waterfall. Beside the water that fell was a little antique house painted in red with a red roof. The shadow of the house reflected on the surface of that nature window. I wondered who could paint this giant creation?

Phu

What Makes Me Happy?

Just being alive
When I see my family
When I'm able to call home
Seeing birds flying
Playing basketball
Reading to myself
Listening to soft music
When my kids hug me
When I'm showering
Telling my kids I love them
Knowing my release date is almost here.

Eddie

Thoughts On Friendship

Just knowing that your thoughts are with me warms my heart when I am cold. Remembering your gentle smile soothes always my loneliness. The miles between us keep us strong, a strength that brings visions of times yet to be, sharing by special friends like us.

Sometimes I wish you would tell me what you're thinking, no matter how sad or angry. For even though I like to laugh with you, we shouldn't hide behind a smile when things are wrong. I care for you whether you're happy or sad. I'm your friend.

Friendship defies age and ignores distance. It weathers the hard times and shares the good. Together we have found this. Our friendship has provided acceptance and understanding in a world that pushes people apart. But I will always remain with the memories of the times we have shared, knowing how fortunate I am to be able to call you my friend... and wife... dear one.

William

Listening To This Music

Listening to this music of a piano being played, unlocking my mind only to enrich my soul with plenty of new ideas. I sit here and ponder, looking around, saying to myself here I am in this place again, in the presence of everyone participating in this class, with me feeling a bit light headed and open minded. My imagination is very far from here although the presence of other people is near. I still hesitate but only to think a far off thought!

Juan

Memories Of A Great Man

Good people make a difference in this world we live in. Dr. Martin Luther King has really been the man that I have always admired, what he stood for. Growing up in the 50's, I can honestly say if it hadn't been for Dr. King believing, there's no telling what this world would have turned to. We still have a long way to go because we still live in a world of ignorance. I truly believe that there is another man who has the same heart Dr. King had. And who knows, I might be that man.

Eddie

Out Of Sight And Mind*

Since I've been in prison I've learned many things. People seem to forget you. Somehow you become nothing. Many people support you at the beginning of your time, then they start to fade away, out of sight, out of mind.

Many make promises they know they can't keep. Some even lie about things on the street. People at home don't know about the life we live, only what they hear and assume. Not knowing it's really like hell sitting in your prison cell, all day and all night, thinking of your future goals and family, watching them fade year after year as you do time. Out of sight, out of mind.

*This became the title for our writing anthology.

William

43

Shell

Shell, where did you come from? The Atlantic, Gulf of Mexico, or the Pacific? What secrets are told behind your ancient coral hard shell back? Maybe the mysteries of Spanish ships that sailed across the great ocean.

Cub

The shell that I hold in my hands looks like a snail that was frightened of getting hurt by a harmful creature. He just curled up to protect himself, but never uncurled. All living creatures have some kind of reaction to protecting themselves when danger comes. So the shell just curls up.

Barry

Feather

The feather reminds me of the big birds at Fort Lauderdale beach. They fly above the ocean, and the people stand up and look at the birds so high in the air they look like small airplanes. When they come down, their wings are so big and snowy white. You can't tame a seagull.

Elijah

When I see a big feather I think of Indians. The way Indians sit together, young ones and old ones. And the hat with all the feathers on it. It is so pretty. And when the Indians are having a party, they light a burning fire and everybody in the teepees are out gathering around the fire. Singing their song. Halla halla.

Barry

The Essence Exercise

If I were an animal, I would be a Platypus because it's a combination of different animals.

If I were a musical instrument, I'd be a one-man band, because music tames the beast in us all.

If I were an article of clothing, I'd be a sweater, so I could keep a person warm.

If I were a mode of transportation, I'd be a bus, because a bus holds a lot of people.

If I were a type of weather, I'd be the sun, because it's warm and you need it, plants need it, animals need it, and it's a gift from God.

If I were a book, my title would be *The Life and Times of Me,* because having this title would include everybody who reads it.

James

The Essence Exercise

If I were an animal, I would be a fish because I could swim the deepest depths of the ocean, never before explored.

If I were a musical instrument, I'd be a flute, because every breath of air that was blown through I would capture and make a beautiful sound out of it.

If I were an article of clothing, I'd be a coat, because I could cover someone with a lot of warmth.

If I were a mode of transportation, I'd be a plane, because it would give me the strength of a bird flying freely, only to hold you in my comfort.

If I were a type of weather, I'd be a summer rain. My rain drops would fall all around you, and upon you, only to cover the foundation of the earth, making it more plentiful.

If I were a book, my title would be: *Life Spins,* because life often has us wondering what's going to happen next, just like a whirlwind.

Juan

POETRY

I AM Poems

This is another example of an I AM poem, which comes with its own structure. For the starting line, "I am," the writer must think of two qualities. Then that line is repeated as a last line of all stanzas, acting as a "chorus." The prompts that follow: "I wonder, I hear, I see," etc. give students the opportunity to fill in the blanks. I have included my own I AM poem at the end.

I AM

I am a lonely guy under the tree
I wonder how life would be if I could stop the seasons from changing?
I hear the wind blow by
I see the leaves fall, because of fall
I want to hold the season
I am a lonely guy under the tree.

I pretend I'm in love
I feel the love of the wind on my face
I touch the warmth of the wind that is leaving me
I worry it won't last
I cry if it goes
I am a lonely guy under the tree.

I understand that you must go
I say that I understand
I dream to make it real
I try to imagine that moment
I hope it can come true
I am a lonely guy under the tree.

Phu

47

I AM

I am a troublesome man who has a lot of feelings
I wonder what life would be like without pain
I hear a lot of people crying
I see a lot of emotions
I want a better world for everyone
I am a troublesome man who has a lot of feelings

I pretend to be a god of love
I feel all pain that runs through other people's minds
I touch the heart of many people across the world
I worry about when the world is going to end
I cry when people die
I am a troublesome man who has a lot of feelings.

(The poem ended here.)

Anthony

I AM

I am a literary woman who loves to go barefoot
I wonder when my novel will hit the stands
I hear people clapping at the music of my heart
I see pure crisp pages covered with strong words
I want peace throughout the challenge of time
I am a literary woman who loves to go barefoot.

I pretend I'm wiser than I really am
I feel sorrow for the hungry and abused
I touch your shoulder to let you know I care
I worry my hands can never reach us all
I cry when old friends die
I am a literary woman who loves to go barefoot.

I understand that treasures lie beneath the surface
I say dig deep, climb high
I dream of a world where joy comes every day
I try to be patient with my human frailties
I hope one day to rise above the storm
I am a literary woman who loves to go barefoot.

Katya

Acrostic Poems

I introduce acrostics to provide a structure and a theme for student poems. As you can see from the examples below, the theme (in this case LOVE) is written vertically down the page, and each new line must begin with that letter. Elsewhere in this anthology there will be acrostic poems on other themes.

Love

L istening to the sounds of the birds

O ur hearts and minds wander

V isions of freedom are

E ver upon us

Cub

L isten for the god

O f love to be mine

V oice of freedom for

E verlasting happiness

Anthony

Love

L iving together as husband and wife

O ver the years I have found that it's nice to take a

V acation from work and stress to become an

E verlasting family

Eddie

L etting our feelings run wild

O ver the past of time

V isiting the old and new

E verybody has a life to renew

Cub

L isten

O h do not turn away from the

V oice that's singing to

E ase your sorrow

Katya

Five Noun Poems

This is another example of experimenting with a way to give form to a poem to help the writer organize their images and feelings. (The nouns given were: flower, love, hill, sorrow, and baby.)

A Flower

Walking alone on the road
with a flower in my hand
I came near the hill
by the old oak tree
where sorrow and pain had
gotten the best of me.
Oh, what is that, the cry of
a baby in the wind?
What memories of the
places and people I will always love.

Cub

A Life Of Flowers

Love is so beautiful
knowing that it is real
sometimes it can make you feel sorrow
in other ways it can bring you
a life of flowers
that can blossom on hills or mountains
My, my, just the thought of closeness
makes you want to cry like a baby.

Eddie

Free Verse

This is an example of a poem composed without a given structure or form. I cannot now remember what the assignment was, but this was written by the same student who wrote about his vivid memories of discovering a waterfall and red "antique house" in a small town in China.

Missing My Homeland

Once again, sun sets.
Who's sitting, who's fishing, who's waiting
Who's longing, who's remembering, who's loving?
Along the river, whose boat flows and flutters?
Please send my message to the one I loved,
depicting all my heart and soul.
I am a mourner who must leave to make you grieve.

Phu

Haiku

Who judges my life
when lonely was my domain
I record my self

Phu

Reflections on the Writing Class

Now and then, I ask students to reflect on the benefits of our time together. It gives us all a chance to put into words an experience that may be unique for many of the participants. As for myself, I have never become bored or sated in offering individuals (and myself) a chance to write in the company of others. Every class has a unique chemistry, and each person lends his/her special voice to the collective.

This writing class has brought a bunch of men from many different races and religions together. Inside these walls we must all be on alert at all times from one another, but in this small writing class we are all together as one, as we express our feelings and emotions in this journal. It's funny how a small class like this could bring a bunch of men together to make them better human beings.

Richard

Prison is a world of steel bars, barbed wire, razor wire, brick walls and locked doors. Once a week we are invited to open our minds and feel free to express ourselves. We are able to say and write, instead of listening and doing. If only for a few hours a week, at least in our minds, we are free.

Woodrow

Reflections on the Writing Class

Since my writing teacher has been teaching this class, I didn't know I had so many thoughts in my mind. Whenever she tells me to write about something, I mean anything, it just comes to my mind and before I know it I have written a poem. And that is something I have never done before.

Thank you for everything you have done to refresh my memory and make all my thoughts come out of me.

Barry

This writing class has meant for me an opportunity to look beneath the exterior into the heart and soul of human beings who have because of circumstance or fate ended up behind bars. When we write together I do not feel the bars. I feel sunlight penetrating the walls, lighting up the caves and recesses of our secret inner spaces.

I take our stories with me, like a handful of gemstones. I don't forget all that we have spoken so eloquently here.

Katya

Beauty Behind Walls

A Literary Journal

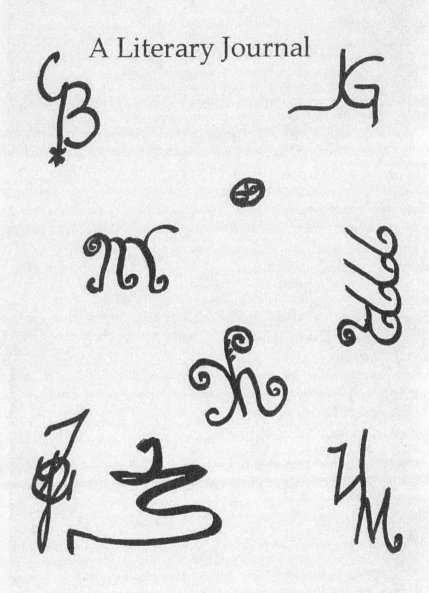

Jefferson Correctional Institution
Fall, 1998

Jefferson Correctional Institution: *Beauty Behind Walls*, 1998

In the Fall of 1998 I was invited to be part of an artist-in-residence grant at Jefferson Correctional Institution, a women's prison in Monticello, Florida. There were four of us included, each with a different set of skills to bring to the inmates. I was chosen to provide yoga and creative movement experiences, as well as the same kind of writing I had been offering at Leon County Jail and the local federal prison. That will explain why there are fewer excerpts from the anthology we put together, due to the wealth of other activities.

The women chose to call their literary review "Beauty Behind Walls." The resident artists came up with the idea that each inmate, and each teacher, should choose a "spiritual" name for the duration of our time together, and so it is these names that appear on each woman's work. (I chose the name Tucson, because my grandmother Baba, who gave me my first diary, lived for many years there.) At some point during our time together, we asked the writers to draw symbols of themselves, which later appeared on the cover of the anthology.

As with the preceding anthologies, all excerpts originate from seed prompts that help evoke student writing.

I Was Born

I was born African American, great granddaughter of slave holders, granddaughter of a living legend run away slave, 103 years old.

I was born in the midst of struggle shortly after the great Depression, 1942, in Lorraine, Ohio, in a little log cabin house full of warmth, love, and God.

I was born to define myself, a Mother, giver of life, a nurturer, with compassion to teach, who prides in being Black, has dignity in culture, and walks with integrity.

I was born African American, to strive for unified determination, to suggest viable solutions that aid our communities, and to save our children from the bureaucratic Criminal Justice Penal System.

I was born to have freedom, the ability to speak with diplomacy, be educated to survive struggle with liberty.

I was *not* born to be locked up in the abyss of loneliness, peering through bars and wire fences.

I was born African American…

Free Spirit

Free Spirit

My Hands

Oh what a gift to be able to hold a loved one, to touch the beauties of the universe. To grab on to a piece of this world. So many miraculous things can be done. For I was blessed, something wonderful, to have such hands.

Angelic

A Favorite Garment

My favorite boots are my Redwings... I walk the swamps with them, balancing on roots beneath ancient cypress in Tate's Hell State Forest. They make me feel courageous, balanced, like a pioneer from ages past... Lewis and Clark...discovering new territories... They carry me miles along the riverbank...bobcats peek at me from behind palmettos...Over fallen trees that make bridges for me to wander deeper into the swamp. My boots lay tracks alongside the turkey and bear tracks...they bring me home...back to my waiting canoe...to the bank...back down the road across the cold...and back to the fire that keeps out the cold... I take my Redwings off and let them rest beside the fire...until tomorrow's trek.

Blueberry

At This Very Moment

At this very moment I feel like reaching to the sky.
I feel wild like the flowers that surround me.
I feel soft like silk.

Star

A Rainy Day

A rainy day makes me want to curl up with a good book, make hot apple cider with a dash of cinnamon, and drink it on my screened-in back porch, sitting in the old wicker rocking chair.

A rainy day makes me want to put on my old rain slicker and my green rubber boots bought in Oregon and go out into my garden to count flowers, to pick up wet twigs, to pluck off the dead blossoms, to run across the street and into the park.

No one is there but me except the squirrels scrambling up the glistening trees, shaking their tails, mouths plump with seeds. No one but the great owl, whose sleep has been disturbed, who shakes her great wings and stares down at me with golden eyes.

I run in the rain, throwing off my hood, and down the water drenches me like a mother's tears...

Tucson

If Laughter Had A Taste

If laughter had a taste it would be as sweet as your smile, as tangy as the dazzling sun that shines for miles and miles. If laughter had a taste it would be as pleasant as surrender, as pleasing to the palate as the touch that I remember....

Pebbles

61

POETRY

One of the poetry prompts I use to evoke creativity from my students is the first line of a Lucille Clifton poem. It begins: "In my 38th year of life" and goes on to exclaim where she, the poet, finds herself. I ask each student to use their own age to create their first line... Here are five examples, including my own. As you will notice, one of my students chose to write her 40th year story in prose.

In My __ Year Of Life

My 31st year, it's the beginning of the new and improved me
For life has been cold and hard you see.
Much has been learned throughout my pain and fears
Lots of hurdles to jump, I've fought back the tears
Today, a woman smart beyond my years.

Angelic

My world becomes centered now
in my forty-fourth year
Heavens have opened before me
and brought forth the joy of the universe.
I see the sparkle of the stars in the eyes of my chosen love
as we glide through the galaxies together, sharing our journey.
We travel into and through the future
riding on the tail of comets
exploring the many colors of the sky.

Pebbles

My 40th Year Of Life

My 40th year of life was not much appreciated, by anyone, not the Prosecutor, or the Court, or the Jury, or much anyone at all. My life, a mixture of opposites: joy, fear, poverty, richness. Elegance, desperation – like a picnic thrown by psychotic gods.

"Here's let's feed her this and see if she can take it."

"Yes, she handled that well, didn't she?"

Miracles, peace in pieces, horror in curtains of rain on my picnic spread by the Gods.

My 40 years of living and pulling my courage up through every day of it. Choosing to survive, to live, to love, to give life… choosing to live another 40 years.

Blueberry

My 26th Year Of Life

In my twenty-sixty year of life
I'm sitting here in prison
trying to focus on getting my life back
on the right track
living, working, exercising,
hoping one day my goal will get here.
I know now what I didn't know then.
Now I can take those tools home
and use them well
not only for me, but my children too.
When I look in the mirror, what do I see?
Beauty!

Cherokee

In My 54th Year Of Life

In my fifty-fourth year of life
I dreamed that I walked into the sunshine and the rain
my cloak unbuttoned
my hands palms opened.
The sacred birds flew down from the trees
to feed me exotic berries
staining my eager lips.
Music followed me like bells on my naked heels,
the path opening like a quiet river
a series of golden stepping stones.
Of course I had with me my journal,
the story of my life, and my favorite pen
filled with the juice of my flesh, bones, and nerves.
In my 54th year of life, my silver hair glowed in the moonlight
and my daughter skipped behind me chanting her magic song...

Tucson

*Now each student wrote down one line from their age poem, we shuffled
and drew, in this order, to create a group poem.*

In This Year Of Our Life

Sacred birds flew down from the trees to feed me exotic berries
The life I live makes my light shine
I have learned to be me
God and angels must have been around
Give me courage to see another year
    to be the person I know in my heart I really am
Today, a woman smart beyond my years
This year, a picnic was thrown by psychotic gods
Help me to learn the right ways to go
    as we glide through the galaxies
To say the words that talk about what we know, forget, know
Fruitful Mother
In this year of life, I look in the mirror and what do I see?
Beauty!

*Composed by: Tucson, Cinderella, Taz, Sunshine, Butterfly, Angelic, Blueberry,
Goodness, Pebbles, Jump, Free Spirit, and Cherokee*

The I AM Poems

As I have already mentioned, in the I AM poems the first line repeats at the end of each stanza, and each woman fills in the blanks, after the opening phrase (i.e. I wonder, I hear, I see, etc.)

I AM

I am a woman of beauty,
I wonder about the beach
I hear the ocean and winds
I see the beautiful flowers
I want to fly like a bird
I am a woman of beauty.

I pretend I'm a cat
I feel soft and cuddly,
I touch the warmness of the heart
I worry about those in need
I cry when it hurts
I am a woman of beauty.

I understand the feelings of sorrow
I say peace, love and happiness,
I dream of a handsome man
I try to keep the feelings mutual
I hope that one day I will have peace, love and happiness
I am a woman of beauty.

Cherokee

I AM

I am a happy, loving person
I wonder if there's more people like me
I hear music in the air
I see me dancing on a cloud
I am a happy, loving person

I pretend to be free
I feel I should be free
I touch the freedom
I cry about freedom
I am a happy, loving woman

I understand love
I say I want to be loved
I dream of being in love
I try to love
I hope to be loved by you,
I am a happy, loving person.

Teal

I AM

I am patiently walking my life path, learning every step
I wonder if I was an oak on this path in a previous life
dropping acorns in the path of another's feet
I hear raindrops filtering through the leaves, softening
my path, voices in the distance urging me on.
I see shadows of my future slip like ghosts in the mist,
haunting memories hang in heavy, moss-draped branches
I want this path to end in peace and joy

I am patiently walking my life path, learning every step.
I pretend the shadows do not frighten me, to be braver
 than I am
I feel alone, quiet,
I touch the leaves as I pass, huckleberry, magnolia, holly
I worry about nothing, I empty my mind and open my spirit
I cry about the good things I've experienced and missed
I am patiently walking my life path, learning every step.

I understand the path is hard, but the journey is good
I say the words that design my life path
I dream my future, my past
I try to make the path clearer for those coming behind me
I look for signs of those who have gone before me
I hope my path ends in prosperity of heart and mind,
in joy of life
I am patiently walking my life path, learning every step.

Blueberry

Blueberry

A Woman Made Whole

Once my proud father's little princess
My bragging mother's brightest child
A nothing to myself
I had no inner style
I cook, I clean
My days are filled with strife
A lover, a friend
Now somebody's wife

A prison number
Now my name
Smoking drugs, someone's trick
Caught up in the game
My family, my friends to behold
I'm a nobody I feel
Gone is my inner soul

Always someone's something
Today I am on my own
I've made it, it's been hard
Through this journey, me and me alone
I found myself
I now have a goal
I am strong, no longer weak
Angelic, a woman made whole.

Angelic

Over the many years of offering writing classes, I often find myself coming up with new seed phrases, and exercises, both to stimulate new material from my students but also to challenge myself. The following seven anthologies, all the work of women at FCI, Tallahassee, will introduce three new forms, all of which rely on the writer's imagination to fulfill. I have long felt that fiction is another avenue for revealing our many-layered selves, and that a made-up or make-believe story can be as revelatory as a story based on so-called "fact." Here are the three prompts.

Once upon a time, a seed story: After writing together for an hour or so, I pass out cards and ask my students to write one phrase from their work that day—three or four words maximum. For example, someone may write *"she taught me"* or *"love filled the air."* We gather all the cards, I shuffle them, then ask three people in the class to pick one from the mix. Once we have the three phrases, students are told to incorporate them into their fable, which will start with the words *Once upon a time...*

I enter the scene: I pass out calendar pictures of scenes from nature (mountains, waterfalls, trees, flowers, etc.). Often these images are pasted on the cover of the women's writing journals. I ask students to "go into" the landscape—to sit by the river, to smell the flowers, to hike the mountain, for example. Students seem to have no trouble at all imagining themselves in the middle of a beautiful place. Their writing flourishes, as you shall see.

Two Noun stories: Students choose a partner. Each independently comes up with a noun (one says *rain*, the other says *slipper*), they put the two nouns together—*Rain Slipper*—and each writes her own story based on the title. Once they have finished, they share their stories with one another. No two stories are ever alike—some are totally fiction; others are partly true, partly fiction; some are based on real experiences in their lives.

Imagination is a fuel that heightens our experience of ourselves as writers, helps us create new realities and is also lots of fun!

IMAGINATIONS UNCOVERED

The Stories of Women
from Tallahassee Correctional Institution
Autumn, 2010

FCI Women: *Imaginations Uncovered,* 2010

I took time away from teaching inmate classes to work on several book projects and to offer writing courses in the local community. By the time I was ready to offer inmate classes again, FCI had become a women's prison. I met the Education Program Director, Beth Nichols, and she was very supportive in bringing me in to teach Lifestories again. I asked the women in that class to come up with a name for our anthology, and they chose "Imaginations Uncovered." (Cover graphic by Janelle.) As always, we write from evocative seed phrases. On rare occasion, the student chooses her own title (i.e. There Are Days).

I Remember A Room

The room was large and spacey with high ceilings from which echoes sound from a deafening intercom. People were buzzing in and out, some appear sad, some happy. But for me, I was anxious. For the previous days anxiety was getting the best of me. I tried to calm my nerves but my friends wouldn't allow me. They didn't understand. They had their father all of their lives. So how could they? For me it was different.

I escaped their presence to console myself. I needed this time alone. Not acting selfishly, I drifted off to a large window. From this vantage point I was able to absorb myself into the view of flights taking off and landing and men fueling airplanes. I even absorbed myself further, taking in the ocean's blue water.

In the midst of my solace, I recalled from a younger age, how people always kept saying I resembled my father. Now today I was about to see.

In a hush of silence, I paced back to the presence of my waiting friends. They greeted me with smiling faces and curiosity sparking in their eyes. "They may know something I don't," I said to myself.

Then all at once, a large two-sided glass door burst open. All eyes turned towards the door. I followed in pursuit to behold a tall, handsome light skinned man with wavy black hair, decked out in suit and tie, emerge from beyond the door.

One look at this man and I knew he was my true blood, my strength from whence I cometh. I never had to second-guess. I stepped forward. The man dropped his bag, rushed to me and without one word said, we embraced into locked arms.

He was my father, the man I never once heard his voice nor saw his face. He was the man I so longed to behold and never had that chance until then, nineteen years after I was born. Now finally I was locked in my father's arms. I will never forget this room.

Linneth

There Are Days

There are days when I awake feeling nothing but pain in my heart, sorrows in my soul and conflict surrounding me.

Incarceration is a situation where everything is going on in depth. One thing I have learned is to keep alive, keep living, keep a beating heart abounding. Strength will be my victory.

Sometimes I Feel

Sometimes I feel like a joy of melody pounding inside of my ears and in my heart.
Sometimes I feel like a butterfly, a radiant colorful one, spreading my wings above high.
Sometimes I feel like a bird flying in the air, high up in the sky.
Sometimes I feel like a fish, a great big dolphin floating on top of the water, playful fishes circling round.
Sometimes I feel like a singer, picking my guitar strings, and making movements to the wonderful beats.
Sometimes I even feel like a strong hurl of wind, whistling between the trees.
Sometimes! Sometimes! Sometimes!
Oh if you ever knew how much I feel.

Linneth

Self Portrait Haiku

Now, I am renewed
once lost, broken and so bruised
today I rise above

So, Here I Am

So, here I am, surrounded by beautiful women. Some mothers, others not. Each belonging to families that miss and love them. The ladies each have their own unique story to tell. I wonder what surprises will develop in the next few hours. Ahh! Creativity, I can hear it beginning to awaken out of its sleep. Rise women and share. Let the beauty of your strengths and weakness emerge. Write!

I Enter The Scene

I enter the scene with love radiating through every part of me. I can smell the autumn season in full bloom. I am reminded of how like the leaves dying, we too must die. Once we shed the weights of the past, the grudges and regrets that we've held on to for so long, we become free. Dying to self is painful and dreary, but produces such life and happiness on the inside.

I take a deep breath and am just happy to be home. My family is near and I am free. The leaves crunch with every step. I reach out to touch one of the beautiful red leaves. Finally, I've made it home. The days seemed to drag at times. But I am better and it was worth pressing on. Now everyday is a dream come true. Home. This is where I belong.

Misty

75

At This Very Moment

At this very moment I realize that all things in life give life to life. I see beauty in the things I thought were not capable. At this very moment love has taken a turn for the best and will result in changes known, unknown, and undecided. At this moment the sounds I hear tell me that the moment is not over but has just begun.

I Remember A Room

I remember a room that held lights. I saw hues of blue and light grey. There was silver and sounds of drumming from machines making melodies of their own. There were people dressed in white talking to me, directing and instructing me. In that room I hurt. I experienced pain, but that all went away after one sound was made that silenced everything else. Yes, I remember a room, a room in which I became a mother.

A Rainy Day

On a rainy day I consider myself blessed that the rain water is one that I can enjoy as a relief from a long day that may have been just a little too hot for my make-up, instead of a day that I've desperately looked forward to because as the water falls I'm underneath its arrival with an aluminum pail I've found to catch the drips, knowing that each drop is more important than the drop before, acknowledging that I need that bucket to fill up in order to quench the thirst of my starving children. See now I'm in a third world country only dreaming of the day that on a rainy day I'll be watching my children play in the water, building mud pies instead of crying because they can't see the floor of their house. It's made of dirt which in turn on a day that should be tranquil is a curse of mud under their feet...

Tabitha

Self Portrait Haiku

Risen above all
life no longer in turmoil
know that I am here

An Old Pair Of Shoes

An old pair of shoes can tell a lot about a person. They could mean the person is too cheap to buy new ones, that they have a lot of money, or maybe the shoes are sentimental somehow. Shoes are just like people to me. Some smell good and others smell bad. They come in different shapes, styles, designs and colors too.

I remember an old pair of shoes that I still have today. I've kept them as a token of appreciation. As a memento of a journey that I've taken. My first pair of combat boots were given to me by a woman with an evil glare and a hat that looked like it belonged to Smokey the Bear. She called herself a Drill Instructor. From the moment my feet slipped into those tan roughed boots I was in another world. A world of new words like attention, dress- right-dress, and platoon halt.

For four years, those boots traveled with me. They climbed the desert, sandy hills of 29 Palms, CA. They've been hauled through mud, dirt and grime. These boots kept me motivated for company runs that lasted five miles. When I had to hike fifteen miles with a ninety-pound pack, feeling exhausted and worn out, these boots carried me through. They stood proudly with me when I graduated boot camp and was deemed a U.S. Marine. Even after they joined me on a tour to Iraq.

These boots are an extension of me. We've experienced so much together. When I look at those boots all the memories flash through my mind. Together we've seen good and bad, lost some friends, and experienced combat. With these boots my life has been forever changed.

Denise

I Remember A Room

I remember a room where love filled the air. A room that gave me peace. With light blue walls and a big open window. The breeze flew in and you could hear birds singing softly outside. A room where I felt safe and secure. Nothing could harm me. There was a bed as comfortable as I imagine it would be to sit on a cloud. A bed full of fluffy blue and white striped pillows. A room where I wrote my first poem, my first words, my first everything. A room where my mom gave me so much wisdom. A place I could share all my secrets and they wouldn't be heard. A room that was another part of me.

Sometimes I Find Myself Thinking

Sometimes I find myself thinking, why am I really here? What is my purpose in life? Isn't that what we all long for? To know our purpose is to have some sense of direction. Tossed by the waves of trouble and despair, we find ourselves lost in another realm.

I find myself thinking "what if" to everything. You realize the extensive power of a simple choice. Everything can change in a moment of decision.

I find myself wishing I could turn back time to fix things and make the outcomes perfect in my eyes. I'm always looking for concrete answers when most of the time there aren't any.

Sometimes I wonder if thinking so much could drive a person crazy. Maybe I'm already there. What's a girl to do?

Denise

So, Here I Am

So, here I am, facing another day with greater expectations, learning and understanding that my failures have led to my greatest success. Just look at me. I am brilliant, fabulous, and talented so yay here I am. Making sure that I create my own history. I am loving my self, understanding my life, and God's purpose for me in this life. You know the me that is comfortable in her own skin, the me that is secure about who I am. So yay world here I am and if you don't understand me, away you can go… shoo fly don't bother me.

If I Had The Time

If I had the time, I would travel all over the world. I would go meet this His Holiness the Dalai Lama and tell him of the times I dreamed of the very day that I would shake his hand.

Then I'd go over to Africa to meet Nelson Mandela just to let him know that I think he is a great man, and how watching what he endured and how so many things because of him have changed.

Then I'd go over to India to eat with a swami and hear all the Hindu stories, and watch a beautiful sunset.

I would ride a camel to Mecca just to have a view of their gorgeous mosque. And then I'd take a dip in the river of Jordan, and allow the waters to bless me.

I would love to see where exactly did King Tut live, because I know the pyramids are an awesome scene.

I would love to talk to a Holocaust Survivor so that I can say the right words to help relieve some of their pain.

Or maybe meet a Samurai warrior and learn his technique.

So the question is, if I had the time, where wouldn't I be?

Latavia

I Enter The Scene

I enter the scene and I know how beauty feels. It's soft and delicate. It's bold and brilliant. How do I feel bold-brilliance you ask? It's warmth exuding. It's a breathtaking dream that says come and rest, soak me in, you belong here. I'm looking around to others to enter the scene, and it's taking them in …

Self Portrait Haiku

Define who I am
A glimmer of the great I AM
from darkness to light

Heart so filled with life
great, humble, rich and poor still
mysterious treasure

Today

Today she opened her mouth and spoke from her heart. No grand adventure for most but for her, it felt like a leap. She took a chance and shared what seemed to be burdening her into a corner with no real relief in sight. Before today, quitting appeared as the go-to option to relieve the stress of continuing with no direction. No one knows the story behind the daily smile.

A song played in her heart, "I feel like going on," so she opened her mouth and spoke. Surprisingly, someone was there to listen, genuinely. Someone had always been listening, she just hadn't risen to the challenge of speaking until right now.

KeLana

If My Life Were A Book

If my life were a book it would be a book of poetry. There's so much to tell and so many stories that need to be heard that sometimes the most profound story is only in a few words. Poetry has always been the way to a heart's diary. Some of the most tender feelings are captured in rhythm. What would make my story so different from the next person with a similar story? Nothing, only the way it's told.

I Remember A Room

I remember a room at the hospital where my son Jewelz was born. I had the most tremendous view from a window that was as big as the wall. It was sunrise and the sky was red, pink and orange. There was mist coming over mountains. I was alone except for a small bundle wrapped in my arms. So beautiful. That room through all the turmoil that was currently in my life gave me the most meaningful, peaceful morning of my life. There was an officer outside my door...

Today In The Third Person

Today she just wanted to rest. Her life was no longer becoming her own. She had become so busy she was actually overwhelmed. She just wanted to do something her own body didn't want her to. She went to sleep. She put earplugs in her ears and a sleep mask over her eyes and drifted to the one place she knew had solitude, her dreams.

It didn't take long before the all white dormitory became a scene of darkness waiting to be filled with the colors of her imagination. The noise of her surroundings became replaced by quietness that the Lord knew she most desperately needed. No one knows exactly when a brain starts to create its images but it must have come upon her rather quickly. She dreamed of New York City, walking down the busy streets of her beloved Manhattan. She looked down on her feet...

Janelle

It Was The Night Of The Full Moon

It was the night of the full moon. I sat outside to admire the starry night. Pegasus showed himself in a beautiful constellation of stars that reflected his power and glory.

As I gazed skyward, I imagined what it would be like to go for a moonlight ride. I would sit on his bare back as we galloped by the ocean. I could feel his strength as we moved as one.

The smell of the ocean brought its salty fragrance to my nose. I inhaled deeply as I treasured this moment in time.

We rode a little longer, Pegasus and me. He spread his wings and together we flew through the night sky. When we returned to the sandy shore and I dismounted, I watched in wonder as he flew away to take his place in the sky.

Did I dream this wonder? My imagination once again has taken me to a magic place. I will cherish the memory always, until the next journey begins.

Jamie

I Enter The Scene

I enter the scene of a dahlia. My outer petals are a bright fuchsia color. My next layer of petals is canary yellow. My center petals are a slighter shade of yellow with lime green sprouts.

I signify beauty and peace of mind with my brilliant colors. Do you feel my calming power as you gaze and admire me?

I am alive and vibrant and I want you to feel the same as I do. Is your perception of me as intense as my colors? Smell my fragrance. Inhale it so it becomes part of you. May peace and joy fulfill you.

I Am A Woman Who

I am a woman who has used my life to help heal and to see lives change through my tutelage. I have seen those that are battered, beaten and at rock bottom living with the hand life has dealt them. I have seen them triumph over their burdens and see that love is in the air. They are not alone…

These people learn to create something beautiful from within themselves. Those that conquer their demons go on to help others as they were helped. Giving of oneself is the key to a happy and fulfilling life. We are all survivors in one way or another.

Jamie

So, Here I Am

So, here I am, finally at peace with who God has made me. Not really concerned anymore with what people think. It is so true, one day people love you, then the next day they hate you.

My heart flows over, full, deep, passionate, colorful and excited about my new beginning. I thought I dreaded the door closing, only to realize a destiny had begun. Here I am.

I Need

I need to tell a story. It excites me to weave a tale of love, betrayal, discovery or fear. When I tell a story, I want the reader to cry when I cried, laugh when I laughed. Ah yes, it is the telling of the story that fulfills my longing soul.

A Day By The Sea

A day by the sea can make the mind plunge deep into the ocean's floor, yet rise and coast along the billowing waves as it hits the silky sands shores.

The sea is the abyss the mind yearns for, but never truly attains because the hourglass of life does not permit the time. That time needed to purge and cleanse. That time needed to inhale and release all that a day can bring. Aha, a day by the sea.

Jewel

At This Very Moment

At this very moment, I feel blessed and lucky to be able to take advantage of doing something that I truly enjoy. I truly believe that everyone comes together somehow if you have faith in yourself and others. This class will be an excellent experience and opportunity to gather most of my thoughts daily as they come. I am certain that I will learn many wonderful lessons as the weeks pass.

It Was The Night Of The Full Moon

It was the night of the full moon when she first felt that yearning to escape and run wildly towards the forest. The feeling stirred deep inside but it had no name. It was desire mixed with fear of the unknown. She felt herself changing but could not pinpoint exactly what they change was.

She walks nervously towards her long mirror behind her bedroom door and is in total shock at what she sees. She is horrible and frightening looking. The dark hair all over, her eyes turning yellow. The long and sharp claws emitting from both her fingers and toes. She realizes her face elongating and the terrifying canine teeth protruding out of her mouth. She jerks back and tries to scream, but all that comes out is a loud howling sound.

She takes a moment to look again at her reflection in the mirror and finally sees what she has become that night of the full moon, and remembers that passionate love bite her boyfriend gave her the night before....

Hands Haiku

Tiny little hands
soft with strength and capable
to change this lost world

Loaisa

Lost in a World

Unexpectedly I get instantly lost in a world only few can understand. My world!!!

The house around me vanishes in a quickness... My deepest thoughts reveal themselves. Changes within myself switch up, questioning each thought that now passes on by!

Looking and searching for some type of answer, viewing it all from all aspects on top of each moment's thought.... I wonder if this is all normal!

My Emotions

My emotions slide down to my heart like a melting candle. Lying here in the dark, my mind's steady running and tears from deep inside roll down this smile I can no longer hold!

Worries and all wonders instantly unfold as I lay behind these walls. Knowing this situation, I somehow chose. Now I'm here trying to understand each emotional blow!

Happiness

Happiness flutters through me
I can't quite explain
a smile goes a long way

DeAnna (Nanz)

I Remember A Room

I see the white walls and hear the music playing on the T.V. The room is filled with doctors and the people I love the most. There's a bed in the middle of the room. In that bed lays a young girl the age of sixteen. The doctors tell me to push. I look over at my husband with tears of pain and joy. My ears hear this wonderful song. It's my healthy little bundle of joy, coming into this cruel world.

I look down at the five pounds and 12 ounce brave soul, and feel my husband squeeze my hand. I look up at him and tell him that I'm scared. My husband asks me what am I scared of? I said making my mother's mistakes… as I look down at this small but mighty miracle.

I Need

I need strength to get me through the days when I see the world through my tears. I need strength for myself so as the days turn into nights I can look at myself in the mirror without hating myself. I need strength so I don't fall back to my old ways.

I need courage to start out the day and take in the ways of being different is okay. To walk on life's roads with my head held high. Not because I'm better than people but held high as in being comfortable with myself as a person.

I need courage to admit that I'm not always right. But to speak out when I feel strongly about something or someone. I need courage on not giving up on being free. I need strength and courage to grow from a child to a young lady.

Christine

If My Life Were A Book

If my life were a book it would be filled with hard lessons learned as a child. My book would tell about being different and growing up unwanted. The pain from a child to the abuse of a battered soul. This book would tell the dreams I had as a child. Curses that were passed down from mother to daughter over the generations.

It would have secrets of a young teenage girl. My first crush. It would tell about the nightmares I've had. The sleepless nights of being a teen mom. I'd offer what little advice I've got.

My book would tell about the great people I've met and even the not-so-great. I'd tell you about my mistakes and my accomplishments. About my heartbreaks and friendships I have had. The friends that are true and even those untrue ones.

My book would have different color pages due to each phase I've been through. Some pages would have smiley faces, others would be tear-stained. It would have pictures of sunrises and sunsets, pictures of the starry sky and the moonlight.

It would have pictures of my children, my brothers, my sisters, and my mother and father. Then it would have a picture of all my family since blood doesn't always mean family.

It would also have my favorite sayings, some I wrote, and others written by other people. My book would be one of a kind like me.

My book would not have an ending since I'm still alive.

Christine

Autumn Leaf Haiku

One magic moment
in the autumn air it fell
rippling in the pond

Old Hands Haiku

Soft, small and dainty
stiffness, pain, inflammation
the work gets done well

Self Portrait Haiku

Just at that moment
as I opened my third eye
spirit in disguise

Ana

Once I Traveled

Once I traveled to an unknown planet. I was sitting in the backyard under a clear black sky showing off its treasure of sparkling tiny diamonds.

I had taken my dogs outside for their usually 11:00 PM outing. They were happy running around chasing each other. I felt comfortable and relaxed and closed my eyes.

Up high in the sky between two stars I saw a yellow-golden light that slowly started descending and hovering a few feet above my head. Suddenly, it looked as if it were glowing, displaying the most intense green, red and orange colored lights. At that moment I wished that they would take me with them.

As I finished my thought I felt as if I was in an invisible vacuum, sucking me up. Within minutes I was viewing from a space ship window a green land filled with gorgeous flowers – red, passion pink, orange, violet and yellow roses, larger and brighter than sunflowers.

Further away I visualized a strange shaped building. It was made out of deep red bricks, flat with many glass windows like doors from where little beings were flowing out. They were adorable, about three feet tall, wearing a white piece of cloth around their pelvic area. They had very light skin, white hair and huge green almond-shaped eyes that looked at me as curiously as I was looking at them.

Slowly the vision started fading, and far away I heard dogs barking. The barking got louder and louder and when I opened my eyes, I was back sitting in the yard, all my five dogs sitting in front of me barking as if they were telling me: "Stop dreaming, Mom, and let's go in to bed."

Ana

Once There Was A Princess

Once there was a princess who lived in a castle at the edge of a forest. One day she was looking out her window down at the snow that had fallen the night before. It was bright, and the air was crisp. She loved the snow. Snow put icicles on all the ledges of the castle. She loved to go out and make snowmen, snow angels, and throw snowballs with the servants.

The princess put on her beautiful white deerskin leather trench coat, with matching snow boots and gloves, with a fancy snow cap, and drew over her head the hood connected to the doeskin leather coat. She grabbed her skis and went out to go cross-country skiing.

As she was enjoying herself, she came upon another set of ski tracks and decided to follow them. She didn't go far when she came upon a man sitting next to a fire, eating. She gazed at him, for he was very masculine. The man felt a presence and looked up right into her eyes. Both of them were startled at each other's appearance. Their eyes said so much to each other, though they'd never met before.

The man stood without breaking eye contact and smiled at the princess. As the princess smiled back, blushing, she was thinking, "My, he's so handsome with a welcoming smile."

The man spoke, "I always wanted to see your face; you are more beautiful than I have heard. I come by frequently wanting to catch a glimpse. Sorry, excuse me, please allow me to introduce myself.

My name is Reynen."

Princess invited him to cross-country ski with her on the trail she frequented and see her to the castle. Princess didn't want to leave his presence, but did have to continue on her way. Princess was ecstatic when Reynen agreed! She hoped he couldn't tell. Reynen was ecstatic also, and also hoped that Princess could not tell either.

As they skied, they both were so nervous they talked about everything and anything. Soon the trail disappeared and the castle was right in front of them. Startled, they laughed, because they didn't even realize they had been standing in front of the castle, talking, laughing, having a whole jolly of a time.

The King, Queen, and all the servants listened and didn't disturb Princess' banter. As Princess and Reynen said their farewells, they gazed into each other's eyes, saying more than what was said, both hoping, but not saying, to see one another again.

Reynen watched Princess enter the castle, hoping she'd glance back before the door closed. She did. Smiling shyly, she closed the door, then leaned against it, sighing deeply, hoping Reynen was sighing just the same. He was.

I Find Myself In A Room

I find myself in a room I've never been before. This room has colors all around. There are five walls. Each wall is painted a different color: blue-green or peacock, fuchsia, lime-green, violet and red-orange. On the blue-green wall there are painted mountains with eagle nests and eagles soaring. On the fuchsia wall there are wild rose bushes of all roses' colors, some made-up, like black and turquoise. On the lime-green wall there are space ships and cute aliens with a black sky and stars. On the violet wall there are wild animals, like snow leopards, white tigers and zebras. On the red-orange wall there are painted all things relating to sports. Especially basketball, like Jordan Jump Man, basketballs, an outside court on top of a hill.

I have a king sized water bed in the center of the room, white couches all along the walls with colorful pillows all over, and windows overlooking evergreen trees and mountains.

Roseen

92

At This Very Moment

At this very moment I'm sitting in a well-lit classroom, surrounded by women who are beginning their own writing journey. On a cool yet sunny October noontime, we all wonder where this four-part workshop adventure will take us. At this very moment, the earth is turning, clouds float in the sky, and a Canada goose struts on the grounds of the prison, free to fly, honking, to its home on a pond…

Once Upon A Time – A Seed Story

(Love filled the air, see lives change, create something beautiful, blessed and lucky)

Once upon a time, long long ago, when people still lived in caves and great tall birds ruled the earth, a young girl – her name was Molly – decided to leave the cave and have an adventure. She took her blessed and lucky stone, carved by her mother into the shape of a star, and crept at dawn out into the world. As a tall bird with purple wings approached, Molly, too innocent to be afraid, asked if she could climb upon his back, and would he please take her far far away to a land where love filled the air. Mr. Bird croaked gently at Molly. "I like to see lives change. I will do as you ask."

Molly and the bird flew high into the October sky, a hint of delicious coolness ruffling Molly's thick brown curly hair. Mr. Bird landed by what appeared to Molly to be the end of the earth, a vast body of water called the ocean. On the shore she found herself taking her mother's precious stone, and drawing on the sand, making swirls and lines and more swirls and more lines. She knew she wanted to create something beautiful. And indeed, with her innocence and adventurous spirit, Molly had invented the alphabet.

Katya

Sometimes I Forget

Sometimes I forget that living is enough. It is not about what I do, or don't do, during the day, whether I am productive enough, creative enough, cheerful enough, focused enough, generous enough, thoughtful enough, or any other measuring system or tabulation to suggest I have earned my worth, my keep....

One is not called to judge oneself as to whether one has earned one's daily bread. One is not being judged by a loving and forgiving god or goddess or the intelligent center of a creative universe. Sometimes I forget that. Sometimes I forget to notice the unending marvels and challenges and intensity and peace of this existence. Remind me, remind me please. Help me remember not to forget how I fit into the fabric of the universe, as one shining ray, one colorful thread, one voice among many.

Highlight From Today In The Third Person

Today she found herself obsessing over the fact that in just two hours she'd be writing for the last time with her class at FCI. She couldn't get her head around this fact. There was so much more to write, to share, to experience together. There were so many more techniques she wanted to pass on to the women.

As these gloomy thoughts went round and round in her head, she suddenly heard the wild honking of a goose, and looked up in time to see it, neck and wings outstretched, landing on the duck pond. How odd that it was alone - geese usually came in a flock. The goose didn't seem the least perturbed or lonely. She just glided along on the calm green water, enjoying a warm October morning.

Well, the woman thought, if a goose can be grateful just to be here now, I guess I can be too. She picked up her pace, heading home, ready to go to her class, trusting somehow that the group *would* assemble again. All it took was determination and the universe tilting in the direction of her desires. She smiled, and all the trees seemed to lean affectionately towards her as she passed by.

Katya

Reflections On The Writing Class

This class has given me the opportunity to realize that somewhere inside my soul there's a part that wants to create, communicate and teach, and this class has demonstrated that I can do it.

Ana

The class has meant that everyone has different things they write about. I write with my emotions... I've challenged myself to write more. It has meant freedom, freedom that allows my mind to leave these prison walls. It also means that I'm not alone when it comes to writing, it's a bond that could last a lifetime.

Christine

It's been a stirring of sorts, a wake up. At one point I used to write, to release. At one point also as a job but I long since gave up doing it. Lazy – intimidated – whatever my reasons for stopping, this class makes me want to try again. To make some time to say something on paper. Maybe there's a real writer in me.

KeLana

This class has been an outlet from a not so profound surrounding. A way to not feel like an outcast. Because there are others who are just like you.

Janelle

In this writing class I discovered that even in this prison setting, there are other women here like me that have many stories to share with the world. It meant a lot to me for Katya to spend time with us, letting us see that how we feel and what we have to share is just as important to her as it is for us. It has meant a lot to me to have these moments in the day to truly be creative.

Tabitha

At this moment now, the words we've shared will always live, too real to erase.

Katya

Imaginations Uncovered

The Stories of Women
from FCI Tallahassee, Spring 2011

FCI Women: Spring 2011

Again, I was escorted to the Education Building for my second six-week class writing with women at the federal prison in Tallahassee. The cover graphic for this anthology was created by Verona. "The hands write, what the heart feels, what the mind thinks." We already had the name for our digest, created by the class of 2010.

Sometimes I Forget

Sometimes I forget all my cares and burrow down under my covers with a good book.

Sometimes I daydream for hours, remember old days and all the paths I took.

Sometimes I cry when no one's around to see my tears fall.

Sometimes I hold up my head, push back my shoulders, in spite of it all.

Spring, An Acrostic Poem

S omething blooming nearby

P retty flowers of all colors

R ed ones, yellow and blue

I love the bluebonnets the best

N ear the highway I see them covering the hillsides

G iant garden of gumdrops

Amy

A Childhood Friend

Ivory was my childhood friend. We even named ourselves Ebony and Ivory. Our friendship was at a time in our country when race weighed more than friendship. She, Ivory, was white and was expected to play with other white girls and I was colored – that's what they called me back then – and expected to play with other colored girls.

Well, we marched to our own set of rules. We met in first grade and instantly became friends. We were color blind, and didn't understand what all the fuss was about.

Ivory loved to jump rope, and so did I. I loved to play hide and seek, and so did she. Oh the fun we had, running, hiding, climbing, giggling. Ours was an innocent friendship, free of labels, untainted by racism or politics.

Today (In The Third Person)

Today she looked back twenty-seven years. She remembered that taxi ride to the hospital. She remembered the first word and steps her daughter took. Oh such a flood of memories of yesterdays took place today. Then she stepped back to now and picked up the phone to call her daughter. In her head, she was thinking what would she say? Instantly, her daughter picked up the phone and the woman did what she naturally did for 27 years. She sang Happy Birthday!

Sometimes I Wish

Sometimes I wish I could turn back the hands of time. I would have listened to my father and used all of his wonderful advice he would share with me. I wish I had lived my life differently, that my heart would have stayed pure. I wish I could be the little me again and know what I know now. Oh how I wish…

Pauline

I Enter The Scene

From a calendar picture.

I enter the scene... It's beautiful. I'm back home in Kansas, where the sunflowers surround the grass. The sky is clear, and birds are singing. It feels so real. Fresh air fills my nose. My children are running around chasing each other. It's nice to be back where the sunflowers grow and the skies are clear and beautiful. It feels so good to be home.

Ten Years Ago

Ten years ago, I was 19 and just starting life. I moved out with a close girlfriend of mine, only to find out it would be hard. It was a struggle for two young women. I was fresh out of high school, working as a cook at Burger King and the other girl was a drop-out working for McDonalds. With both paychecks we could barely pay bills on time. But we wanted and chose to move out of our homes with our parents.

Ten years ago I became pregnant with my first child. Later on I stopped working because the morning sickness was kicking in, and I was extremely tired on most days. So that left one paycheck to pay bills. We made it work out. My friend's mom and dad helped out a lot.

My son's dad disappeared soon as he heard the word "pregnant." Ten years ago I'd fall for anything, because I was young and not full of wisdom. I'm wiser now, ten years later.

Latisha

Name Acrostic Poem

L oving and kind

A ttentive at times

T oday this woman is truly blessed

I s striving for success

S he won't settle for nothing but her best

H eart filled with pain but she maintains

A ll through the days of her life...

Latisha

Sometimes I Wish

Sometimes I wish I could start my whole life over, beginning as a newborn, fresh into this mucked old world, not aware of all the pains and troubles that lay ahead of me. Feeling so carefree with no worries about anything. Being held with so much love in my mother's arms, feeling the joy of being a baby. Sometimes I wish I could be so different. I would never have chosen the path that I did. I would never have caused my family members so much pain. I would never have done the things that have caused me to be away from my children, not even for one minute.

My Fantasy Vacation

I've always thought of a fantasy vacation being in a place I never dreamed I would be. Somewhere on an island with all my family members around me, on an island with beautiful palm trees, wind sand and blue waters.

There would be a three story house with ten bedrooms, five bathrooms, three living rooms, two dining rooms, three kitchens and a theater room. It would also have a game room as well as a big storage area with every kind of food that you can imagine, and plenty of seafood.

There would be a live band so we can dance the night away! Enjoying ourselves like never before, as if this was our last day to live. I've always thought it would be a beautiful place to be out by the water, looking out. It seems as though we're so far away from everyone else, feeling like we are in a world all by ourselves.

This would be my fantasy vacation, and being with my family – no matter where – as long as we're together. That means the world to me.

Catherine

My Accomplishment

Of all the things I've accomplished, I truly enjoyed going to school. School provided the education I needed to read, write, do math, and other skills needed in everyday life. My good friend from early years dropped out when we reached the eighth grade. However, she never discouraged me from continuing to learn about the world and the many changes in today's modern society. Even when my parents divorced, I was encouraged by my friends and determined to prepare for a job or career along with making my life more rewarding.

Since being in Florida, I've learned even more through schooling such as improving my ability to think rationally, develop such basic values as truth, justice, and my responsibilities as a productive member of society. You see, people throughout the world attend, yet many do not finish, public school, and few people enter college. I was fortunate enough to complete the requirements for each school I've attended. With that knowledge, I'm able to share the joy and encourage as well as motivate others to take advantage of the numerous kinds of schools for people of all ages, and most of all, to complete what they start.

After all, it is said that reading is fundamental, but wisdom—the experience and knowledge, together with being able to apply them—is divine. So do all you can to complete your schooling, there is no greater joy!!

Verona

Verona is the artist who created this anthology's cover art.

I AM

I am Verona that grew from Nikita
I wonder how many others would share what we're in need of
I hear what you're not saying
I see what you're doing
I want to help you without regretting
I am Verona, a woman that grew from Nikita

I pretend that I'm not in need of love
I feel oft times rejected
I touch without the emotional susceptibility
I worry much, yet advance in spite of obstacles
I cry from the heart
I am Verona, a woman that grew from Nikita

I understand with judgment of the situation
I say what I mean
I dream of all the possibilities open to me
I try with a view to success
I hope in the certain things to come
I am Verona, a woman that grew from Nikita.

Verona

I Remember A Room

I remember a room with white walls, and lots of sterilization. I remember the doctor turning me upside down on my head because they lost his heartbeat. I was so scared. What if I ended up being toward him like my mother was toward me? What if he didn't have ten toes or ten fingers, what if he became an inmate or an addict like his mother?

The doctor said push, and I cried. The nurse held my legs up because I couldn't. One more time, I heard the beep of a monitor and the doctor said, "His shoulders are big, a linebacker he will be." And then my son was in my arms.

I trembled so bad. I had to have help to hold him. He was so beautiful. I remember he had no hair, and he was so precious. I remember the pride in my father's voice when I called him to say he had a grandson. I remember this was the first time I ever loved.

If I Were A Poet

If I were a poet
magical beings would play in the sand
Lovers would always walk hand in hand
Peace would reign from nation to nation
and everyday would be a glorious vacation
The wonders of the world would never cease
for every sentence would give life a new lease
Flowers would bloom brighter
and beaches would be whiter
Birds would swing sweeter
and time would have no meter
If I were a poet
no doubt you would know it.

Michelle

Solitude

I seek solitude when reality is too much to bear. It is my escape from life's disappointments, friend's broken promises, a lover's unfaithfulness. Solitude I seek when I can be myself, and not hide behind who I really am, or how I really feel. When I don't have to please anyone else. I seek solitude when my situation gets the best of me, and I feel like I can't make it another day. I seek solitude when I think about my days away from my loved ones, and reflect on how I got here. I seek solitude to work on me, to be a better mother, daughter, and a productive member of society. I seek solitude and will be able to look back and say I made it through.

If I Lived To Be 100

If I live to be 100, I would see my children have children. I'd travel the world, and share my wisdom of life's lessons. If I lived to be 100 I would buy land and sit in my rocking chair on my wooden deck porch, and smile as my grandchildren ran around and enjoyed life. If I lived to be 100 it would be a life of happy memories, and a few heartaches, but what it would be is a true blessing from God.

If I Had The Time

If I had the time, I would make all my wrongs right
If I had the time, I would revisit my childhood and live out all
my dreams
If I had the time I would never miss a second without my kids
If I had the time I would never be where I am today.

Mickeeta

I Remember A Room

I remember a room in Chunchula, Alabama, where my family tells me that I was born in January of nineteen hundred and fifty six, where I was delivered by a midwife. This same room is where my great grandfather died at the age of one hundred and four years old. I don't remember being born in this room, because, like I say, I was a baby, but I sure do remember being in this room with my great grandfather when he died.

I Enter The Scene

From a calendar picture.

I enter the scene, wow! Laying here under this green tree with so many leaves and branches that give me shade, laying on the green grass looking up above me at the clouds and the heavens of God's Creation, just looking and taking in the beauty of it all, letting my eyes roam, seeing the hillsides in the distance, as I lay here and float my mind just free of all worries and all cares of this world.

Oh what peace, laying here under this tree.

Name Acrostic Poem

S imply beautiful and blessed

H appy to be alive and free

E ager to serve

R elaxed within myself

R eal to the bone

Y ou'll love me if you get to know me.

Sherry

If I Live To Be 100

Just the thought of being able to be on earth for a hundred years is a remarkable thought. Knowledge is power! I think of the ways that I can cultivate and mold my future grandchildren and great grandchildren. The knowledge that I can share and the ability to watch how the generations process and utilize, will be amazing…

Even though every child is special and unique in his/her own way, having a great grandparent is like having a blueprint to your soul.

I associate this with the way I love and cherish (study) my own children. If I live to be a hundred years old, my claim to fame would be being the world's greatest great, maybe great-great grandmother.

Name Acrostic Poem

S ensational person

T errific friend

A lways have a smile and

R ich, kind word for a

R eal friend or foe.

Starr

Live Life To The Fullest

Live Life to the fullest, walk into your Destiny
Motivation, determination is authentic
Tear down those old pictures
Put new ones in
You are intellectual

The mind is a terrible thing to waste
Don't wither like the plant without water
Continue to grasp to life,
Focusing balancing and succeeding

When positive thoughts come from the mind
We will be fruitful
When negative thought comes from the mind
We will be unfruitful
So think of fruits on a tree
No water, no fruits; when watered, fruitful.

Allowing your thoughts to control you
The mind is driving you
What you allow in your mind and heart
Is what you think and feel
Imagine a situation in life that you thought about
But allowed the wrong thinking to come to mind
So what you thought wasn't the outcome of the situation
Meaning, your thinking was negative
The situation was positive

What you think and feel determines
your attitude and perspective
It gives a view of self
You become what you think

Don't be like the man that perished away
Stop, think, ask, pray to God to
Lead you to your destiny.
Remember you are worth more
Than gold or silver
Your life has a purpose.

Tora

Once Upon A Time: A Seed Story

(Cool bay waters, looking for fish, excited and nervous)

Once upon a time by the cool bay waters, lived a lonely blue heron. Her kids had grown up and left her to seek their own fortunes and Bella, for that was her name, had found herself in a rut. Standing on one leg, then the other, looking for fish and watching the sunsets, had become old hat. One day, both excited and nervous, she vowed to discover a whole new lifestyle. Would she become a writer like her great aunt Lucy, a world traveler like her grandfather Walter? She knew she had the motivation to change, just as sure as she felt her strong heart beating in her feathered chest. Opening her beak, Bella cried, "At this very moment I declare I will become a ballerina!" And without ado, she began doing arabesques and plies on the sandy shore.

Shimmering Image From Childhood

My grandmother Rose was an exercise addict long before keeping fit was a public obsession. She was always doing jumping jacks, tramping around the dirt lane that circled the lake where my family had a summer cottage, taking cold showers, and sleeping with her windows open, even in winter in Detroit where my Dad grew up. Well, one time she was visiting us in San Francisco – I might have been ten – and Dad decided we should all drive to Yosemite National Park and take Grandma hiking on what turned out to be a very steep and arduous trail, straight up, to a huge rock called Half Dome. I started complaining about twenty minutes into the hike, and Grandma just laughed. She had a walking stick and she was going at a fast pace, leading Dad, Mom, my brother, and me. She must have been in her middle sixties. When we finally got to the summit, I was panting and huffing and sore all over, and Grandma Rose was just sitting on a rock, as cool as a cucumber saying "My goodness, what took you so long? I will never forget that she got to the top before my Dad who was so sure this was one mountain his Mom could never climb.

Katya

Swan Angel — A Two Noun Story

I have traveled around the world and visited castles, museums, jungle villages, ancient courtyards. I have climbed mountains, crossed deserts, lain in flower strewn meadows. I have danced under full moons and lived through fierce storms, but one image holds sway over all the others, and that is a swan angel I discovered in a tiny graveyard in a small town in Mexico. The statue was made of pure white marble, a swan's body and wings with an angel's face. It stood on the grave of a young girl who had died at the age of five. Her name was Angelina, and her last name, oddly, was Swan. Thus the sculpture her family had chosen. I imagined her mother and father, poor peasants, gathering their pesos to hire the village stonemason to create the memorial. I imagined the tearful unveiling, as, dressed in black, the whole village mourned the premature passing of this beloved being. Angelina, never to be forgotten, a name and a memory I will carry to my own grave. The statue, unlike us, will live forever, always pure, the swan its wings gently hugging its own body, the angel's face aglow with tenderness, so pure it lifts even a sinner's heart.

If I Had The Time Haiku

If I had the time
I'd cherish my life's moments
in clockless rhythms

My Hands Haiku

An old woman's hands
treasuring the memories
of ageless service

Katya

Excerpt From: Six Things I Love To Do

I love to play with my children. There is nothing is this world that compares to the happiness that fills my heart when my children are happy. Whether it's playing outside on a sunny day, or inside on the floor, seeing them happy makes my heart smile. Spending time with my babies is something I've yearned to do for the past six years, and ten months from now I'll be able to. Just the thought of the day when my children and I are together once again is enough to keep me satisfied until then.

I AM

I am a beautiful, intelligent woman
I wonder where I'll be in ten years
I hear beautiful birds singing
I see clear blue skies
I want my children in my arms
I am a beautiful, intelligent woman

I pretend I'm a butterfly
I feel so free
I touch my mother's face
I worry about my mother
I cry for my father
I am a beautiful, intelligent woman

I understand that life brings changes
I say live and learn
I dream of being home with my mother and children
I try to maintain sanity in the midst of chaos
I hope my children learn from my mistakes
I am a beautiful, intelligent woman.

Jessica

IMAGINATIONS
UNCOVERED

The Stories Of Women
From FCI Tallahassee, Autumn 2011

FCI Women: Fall 2011

Most often I offer classes in the spring and autumn. So it was that I returned to FCI to begin a new class in the fall of 2011. At that time, no inmate stepped forward to provide the cover graphic. I chose a nature picture from a magazine, similar to the ones I hand out for each woman to paste on her writing journal. I added an open book to remind us all of the "wisdom of the pen."

I Enter The Scene

I am now in the Bahamas. Crooked Island to exact. I feel all the tension ease away as I take in the beauty of the setting sun. The beach is bare. It is as if I am completely and utterly alone in a sacred place. The sound of the water lapping at the shore is a balm for the soul. Here I can look inside and find myself. Here my past holds no meaning, no importance. I am a new creature born in the purity and beauty of the island. Now that the sun has set I find myself wanting to explore the island further. I am surprised to find that there is much excitement among the native. Also to my surprise I find something foreign to me… complete acceptance. I am invited to join in the night's activities. The music is hypnotizing as are the many bodies that are moving in sync. The light of a big bonfire casts shadows that create mystery….

Looking At A Beautiful Scene Haiku

My breath is taken
I am graced by the beauty
my soul is smiling

Vanessa

Sometimes I Feel

Sometimes I feel I can't go on. I don't want to get out of bed or go to work, just stay in bed all day and think some more, hoping to find a solution to make me happy. Then I remember that I have to change my way of thinking if I am to feel better about myself. I must think positive.

Listening To Music

This music reminds me of a Catholic choir, the singing at a funeral of a church member. With the feeling of knowing that he is now in heaven, with no more tears, pain or worrying, feeling free enough to fly.

My Name

I was born in a house by a midwife. I looked so much like my grandfather that I was named Thommie Mae. After awhile my daddy changed my name to Marilyn, spelled like the state of Maryland. I love my name because of the history behind it.

Marilyn

A Happy Memory

It was a beautiful day and we went to the beach to surf. I'd laid out the blankets on the sand and set up the beach chairs. He put on his wet suit and before he reached for his surfboard, he knelt down on one knee next to the chair where I was sitting. He then took my hand and looked deep into my eyes. He lifted my hand to his lips and kissed it. Then, from nowhere, hundreds of seagulls seemed to surround us. They circled above and many landed nearby. He was still looking into my eyes. I looked at the hundreds of sea gulls and looked back at him. He said to me, "My darling, Tamala, would you marry me?" I smiled deeply back at him. My heart was full of warmth. In an instant I said, "Yes." Then just as mysteriously as the sea gulls appeared, they disappeared. I found true love.

A Current Obsession

My current obsession is my tea ceremony. My tea is orange. I steep it hot and let it steep all day covered. Awaiting this moment for the tea ceremony. I always offer my friends to join me. But I prefer my headphones, my crochet, my plate of crackers, and my orange tea. For a brief moment in time I have my tea ceremony. I have myself at home again on my porch, in front of the ocean.

From My I Love To List

I love the salty air in my lungs, the salty water on my skin, the meditation moment, waiting, watching, anticipation. The dolphins swimming around me, as I paddle to the oncoming wave, struggling to reach its peak, catching the peak, feeling the slope of the wave to stand up, catching the wave, feeling the wave, feeling the power of the ocean carrying me, feeling the power of God carrying me, I am free...

Tamala

Sometimes I Feel

Sometimes I feel that I am alone in the world. No one sees me, hears me, nor understands me. Sometimes I feel as though I've been left behind. But what am I really missing? Sometimes I feel as though Peace is within me, until something throws me off balance, and I'm faced with the reality that I do not exist alone.

Sometimes I feel as though I feel too much, which makes me put up my guard, because I don't like to feel sometimes.

Cabin In The Woods, A Visualization

In the cedar chest I pulled out a leather journal. It belonged to my grandmother and in it were letters, thoughts and feelings that she shared with no one except the blank pages in this book. Upon holding it I could feel her presence standing beside me, willing me to open it and discover things about her that I never knew. I randomly flipped through the book and landed on the page titled "The Joys of my Life," and when I scrolled down I saw my name printed in black ink. I smiled and felt a cool air brush over me as if I had been hugged by one of the Joys of my Life.

I Remember A Room

I remember a room in an old house. The room was always cold but it was constantly filled with warmth, love, laughter, good food and good spirits. The room was the kitchen in my grandmother's house. It was the Meeting Room, the Nourishment Room, the Counseling Room, the Gathering Room. The old gas stove not only made the best biscuits and gravy, but also gave us warm heat in the winter. The wooden floorboards would squeak and speak of its age. People always smiled when entering and smiled even bigger when leaving.

Tiffany

I Find Myself In A Room I've Never Been Before...

I find myself in a room I've never been before. The room is big and dark, with only a single file cabinet in it. The only light is the light that highlights my steps as I grow closer to it. The voice I hear is that of my conscience. Slowly and hesitantly I walk towards the cabinet and pull it open. Only one file exists and my name is printed on it. One section is labeled Intention, the second is labeled Thoughts, third is labeled Words, fourth is labeled Actions, and fifth is labeled The Effects Had on People. I pull one card from Intentions and find that my intentions were not always geared towards righteousness. My thoughts were many times shameful. My words hurt a lot of people, my actions not always justified, and I had a stunning effect on a lot of people. The last folder labeled "What will you do?" I decided to walk out of this dark room and live a better life.

So, Here I Am

Here I am in this pleasant place, with these pleasant people, and we've shared our inner thoughts with one another. The air is peaceful, calming, and relaxing, and our spirits are floating high above the clouds.

Tiffany

A Fantasy Vacation

The wind was cool, the sky was clear, the sand was warm between my toes. Looking out at the clear blue water, the umbrella in my drink just added flavor to my day. Oh how peaceful it is to be out by the oceanside. Roll Call!! Oh, well, there goes my fantasy vacation.

Leaf Haiku

The beautiful leaf
it reminds me of myself
we're the same color

Self Portrait Haiku

Oh! Who might I be
old, fragile, gentle and kind
I'm my ancestors

In A Cabin In The Woods I Saw A Cedar Chest...

I was walking in the woods. I came along an old wooden cabin. From the outside looking in it seems no one has lived here in ages. I don't see any furniture though the window. I go around back and the door is ajar, so I step inside. In the back room there's an old cedar chest. I wonder, who could have left it here? I wonder if there's money in it or maybe jewelry. Only one way to find out. I have to open it. So I pray on it, Lord please let this be what I need. You may ask and you shall receive. Well, to my surprise, when I opened this chest, it was just what I wanted. MY LIFE BACK!

April

A Favorite Pair Of Shoes

My most treasured pair of shoes had such a shine! My mother let me pick them out all by myself from the Spiegel's Catalogue. They were the shiniest pair of pink patent leather shoes with a pearl button on the side! We ordered them on a Friday and I waited with such anticipation. Everyday for two weeks I waited for the mailman. When that pair of shoes arrived I felt like queen for a day! I wore those shoes like a second set of feet, it didn't matter if I was going to school or church. I was eight years old…

From My List Of Accomplishments:
Surviving An Abusive Relationship

First let me say it isn't easy. You find yourself wandering back and forth into the same situations, over and over again! Until you decide that you've had enough, when you truly are tired of being broken and sorry and lonely. Then you find the courage and the strength and the desire to want to grow, to believe in yourself, and let go of all the doubt that some sorry man has beat into your head, heart and soul. As time goes by you know with all your heart that you will survive another day and your will gets stronger. You are a survivor. Bring on the victory!!!

When I Look In The Mirror I See

When I look in the mirror I see my mother looking back at me. I have her eyes, her stature in size, and I am able to feel the love that radiates from people around me. When I look in the mirror I see the person God intended me to be, full of life and energy, happy for wonderful me. I may not see a model 5'9," 36-24-36, but I see Mom and Grandma and even Auntie! When I look in the mirror I glimpse the young girl I used to be.

Maria

My Current Obsession

It is a culinary delight, as I take out my bowls, spoon and fork and prepare to whip up a masterpiece! As I open the packages of cream cheese and whip each one with just the right amount of sugar, I slowly add the creamer and hum a song of love, stirring and whipping so that it's just the right texture. Then I add the pudding and the secret ingredient, amazed at the way it fluffs! I add the filling to my already buttery crust and I wait anxiously for it to become chilled. I will share my current obsession with my bunkies, feeling quite content because I know that my secret ingredient is love. If you haven't already guessed, my current obsession is cheesecake. Yum!

I Remember A Room

I have such good feelings when I think about the room. It's on Catherine Street, a half block from the beach. You could feel the breeze from the Atlantic ocean. In this room I gave birth to my three children. Mirrors on the ceiling and such serene peace, the frangipani blossoms outside the window and the scent of night blooming jasmine. The room is my home. It captures you with its atmosphere of "you belong here." In this room you will always feel welcomed.

Maria

I Remember A Room

I remember a room that had a cold feeling in it because the feeling was death. When my little sister was in a coma on her deathbed, and the doctors wanted to take her off the ventilator, my family piped up to see her take her last breath. It was a sad time because the room was so silent with words but you could hear the machines and others breathing. All I could do was take myself to better times I shared with my baby sister and pray to God she was going to a better place. In this room I feel she was comfortable because when the machine stopped she opened her eyes and then took her last breath. It was a relief to her not to suffer any more. When her eyes closed there was a tranquil look on her face. She even smiled, and my aunt said that God had taken her soul with him. I feel now that when I'm in hospital rooms it's not such a bad memory of her. This room is where she spent most of her eleven year life. I have since then enjoyed the vision of being in this room. I loved her dearly and cannot begin to feel lost....

If I Were An Animal

If I were an animal I'd be a lion because they are strong and they are mighty. Lions have courage and wit. I watch how the lioness is when she is watching after her children. She sits back and watches her surroundings and waits to pounce on her prey. I love how the lion family stays together and they are one when they hunt. The father lion has to protect the mother and cubs so he never rests. He has many jobs to do as the man cat.

My Hands Haiku

Small but elegant
my hands have a magic touch
making friends happy

Kadisa

A Favorite Pair Of Shoes

These shoes for me were my Mexican harachis. I bought them at a sidewalk sale in Berkeley, California. They had strong soles made of rubber tires that never wore out, and the leather weave of the shoe itself was flexible and fit my foot perfectly. I wore these shoes day in and day out, with and without socks. I think people probably thought they were the only shoes I owned, but they might as well have been. I even wrote a poem once about my harachis, how when I wore them I felt as if I could fly high above the earth. It was a sad day when the leather straps began to look scruffy, become discolored, and tear. I never found a pair to match them. I'm sure I wore them for more than five years. The stories those shoes could tell!!

I Find Myself In A Room

I find myself in a room I've never been before. It's so quiet I can hear my heart beat. What peace! A chandelier acts as a prism to the sunlight streaming in the two large windows, so rainbows appear on the walls, set to dancing as a breeze blows in through the open door. There's a big round oak table, and on it is an urn of hot coffee and a beautiful porcelain cup. The coffee is strong, the way I like it, so I pour some, sit in the chair and sip and savor the brew. The view is enchanting, palm fronds below, and the ocean is a blue line meeting the sunny sky. A twin bed with pillows is against one wall, and a bookshelf is filled with all the volumes I've been longing to read. I go pick a book off the shelf and realize it's a collection of my short stories. The author's picture on the back cover shows a tanned woman with long white braids, completely at ease, smiling as if just perhaps she is wise.

My Hands Haiku

My hands look like mom's
she's been gone for ten long years
but look, she's with me

Katya

126

Reflections On The Writing Class

I learned how to use my words and express myself. I learned that maybe writing will help me to keep my cool.

Kadisa

This class has been a wonderfully refreshing way to express myself. I was able to open up and be honest about personal trials and situations. I learned from this class that everyone has a voice. Now I know that I do too!

Maria

This class was very inspiring to me. I've learned that there is no wrong way to write about what you're feeling, and that your thoughts are inspiring to others. It has taught me to sit and think about my life.

April

This class allowed me to open up and express my thoughts, feelings and memories that I didn't realize I was capable. It was fun and the environment was always positive. This class encouraged me and made me want to write more. I didn't even know that I could write. Thank you for opening me up. It's easy to shut down in an environment like this. Seeing you every Wednesday made me smile.

Tiffany

I enjoyed this class. It gave me the opportunity to listen to other people's point of view and to share mine. I had a few minutes to feel free and to be myself, which I need to do more often.

Marilyn

IMAGINATIONS
UNCOVERED

Women in Bloom

FCI Tallahassee, Spring, 2012

FCI Women: Spring 2012

I returned to FCI in the spring of 2012, so it made perfect sense to create a cover tying the beauty of the season to the "blooming" of my students. Once again, the icon of the open book completes the image.

In The Middle Of The Night

In the middle of the night I haunt the house because I can't sleep. I would go to my daughter's room just to hear her breathing. I would curl up with a boring book that I have difficulty reading hoping it will put me to sleep. If all else failed, I would go downstairs and vacuum the house. Then pray to God to give me rest, and put my head on my husband's chest.

I Find Myself

I find myself daydreaming. I am sitting on the patio at home enjoying the view of all the beautiful plants that mother has grown. I see the Scotch Bonnet Pepper tree that I planted, and pick a beautiful yellow pepper to put in my soup. I dream of the smell and flavors of homemade cooking and then I come back to prison.

If My Life Were A Book

If my life were a book it would be complete. It would be full of exciting things I dared to do, exciting places I dared to go, exciting men I dared to love, and exciting work I enjoyed. I met many of life's challenges head on, and accomplished most of what I set out to do. I just never thought that my path would lead here. My life's story needs to be expressed, and perhaps the journey was for the best.

At This Moment Now Haiku

At this moment now
I am at peace with the world
happy just to be

Dahlia

When I Look In The Mirror I See

When I look in the mirror I see the authentic self, a woman indeed, I myself and no one else. A kid, a queen, and a woman who dreams. Beautiful indeed, gorgeous as a wedding ring slipped on my finger by my King, yes, I will, I'll be your bride, together as one, keeping our village alive. A mirror, a wall, a family that won't fall.

Self Portrait Haiku

She's re-invented
in the mirror once again
recreated me

If I Were An Animal

If I were an animal, I'd be a member of the sea. Mermaid, skin and scale, with hair of silk smelling of honey and nut, beauty in it self. The Queen of the sea, meeting the shore of the beach at night. Feeling the sand under my feet as I stand ashore like I've come into the world. Soaking and shy as I'm taken away, slipped into a chiffon nightgown. Thank you my love of the sea. As he strokes my hair, I fall asleep. Holding me, I feel his embrace. Tomorrow we'll both return home, to swim with our family. Until we meet again in the sand, on land, we stand hand in hand.'

I Remember A Room

I remember a room filled with a quietness and peacefulness that gave me a sense of self worth. it had a smell of clean linen. And a softness to the touch of my feet, with a sweet fragrance from the sheets.

Lamisha

I Love To

I love to listen to music. I find peace in my radio. Songs are a part of my soul. Lyrics make sense in my mind. Sometimes the noise in my head gets so loud only music can make it quiet. I especially like new rock music. Most people who don't listen to that type of music don't know that it's mostly love songs and songs about pain and hope and life. If you've never tried it, you should.

A Rainy Day

Yesterday was a rainy day. All day was beautiful and dark. I love a fierce storm. When the clouds are dark grey and rolling with the strong winds. It's almost as if God is crying, washing away all of the sin. I fall asleep listening to the rain, then wake in the middle of the night to thunder and pounding and lightning striking. I love a rainy day.

I Remember A Room

My bedroom as a child was dark purple and big. I had my own phone line and stereo. My friends in the neighborhood would come over and we would listen to music and call all of our other friends. My windows were a constant source of trouble because I liked to sneak out at night. My daddy eventually nailed them shut. I didn't like that – at all.

My Name

My name is Star. My daddy gave it to me. He used to always make me feel like I am bright and shining. My hands are his. I love him so much. I miss him even more.

Star*

At This Very Moment

At this very moment I feel highly motivated to take this class, because it's going to be great to have different stories within ourselves that we have lived. This will help my mind to go in space and write every emotion and action I live daily. My teacher is very nice! The flowers inspire me, a lot of peace. Especially today, March 14, 2012, because I had news to confirm my "outdate." I am happy!

I Love To, A List

I love to see the sun
I love to feel the wind on me
I love to be hugged
I love to hear country music
I love to eat munchies
I love to go out shopping
I love to hear the music of Mozart

If I Live To Be 100

If I live to be 100, I would like to have a two- story cake, baby yellow, baby pink with white flowers on it. And a lot of candles! I'd have all of my loved ones around me and have my favorite music playing, so that love's harmony surrounds me and all. I'd have a lot of presents and lots of decorations for my birthday party. There would be many trees outside also decorated for my birthday. Then I'd go out for a walk with my loved ones in the midnight glance of shadows that only the moon will light us up! I'd love to live to see my 100th birthday.

Berta

Sometimes I Wish

Sometimes I wish I could be a bird so I could fly anywhere I desire. The birds and the wind don't have boundaries, and no "races," they only have the best knowledge to nest. I wish I could go to the Amazon and nest in the tallest trees, so when I go somewhere else, no one could find my home. I'd take my little ones with me, upon me, and make them see and understand that even us birds have to sleep. But the rising of a splendid morning is the best that we can see in our eyes as birds along the world.

I Enter The Scene

From a calendar picture.

I enter the scene of these two stunning bright pink flowers. They caught my vision. Only a fool would not admire by heart this love and attraction. I feel the scent of these flowers so close to my face. It feels good to be so loved. When I saw these two flowers together it reminded me of me and you, always till death take us away. So are the flowers. Once they are dead the beauty doesn't exist, but for now, I can only feel love, care, and hold on to everything, because they feel every emotion as we do. They love the rain, the wind, the sun and the water that once in a while I pour to them. Each petal on them is one more we have through all time. They may wilt but come out next season, and always have that bond to earth, just as we do. Each time they shine to the sunlight…is our love.

Berta

At This Very Moment

At this very moment a passion is burning. My life is changing right before me. Everything I know has changed just as my thoughts and feelings have. An undying emotion is brewing within me. This is for sure, I feel truly free. Colors dance in my mind before me as my heart once broken comes whole again. The miracle of life was given to me, and I shall enjoy all its tastes, sounds and visions. In this moment I am truly free.

Sometimes I Forget

Sometimes I forget I am a work of precious art. Every curve, every movement, every emotion, every word are my own. The creator must have smiled when he saw me. A spirit that dreams beyond her limits or boundaries. A wandering soul always looking for people that share her dreams and goals. Sometimes I forget that every rose has its thorn, even within the darkness, she thrives once more. Roots firmly put into the ground and her heart has unbound. A face of an angel and a mind of young thriving scholar as in tune with her scrolls. Always thinking, always growing, always deciding where she will go again. Sometimes I forget that within me lives a person that deserves love, compassion and just friends that truly love her to the end. Sometimes I forget...that the person is me.

Starting Over

Starting over is a statement that breaks up into thoughts of new chapters of one's life. In the written part of my life between the lines I see a dreamer hidden thinking many things that only she knows the answers to. When I open my pen a new wind of change blows through me. A rush of cold water washes away all negative thoughts until I can focus clearly. Starting over is what I dream about when I am free. This new start will be starting there for me.

Rose

I Love To

I love to share positive thoughts with others. There are some days when someone may come up to me and need an encouraging word or I can look at a person's facial expression or action and tell that she is having a bad day. I love to encourage such a person and try my best to instill positiveness into that moment, letting that person know that once there is life, there is hope. With a sense of renewed hope the person will feel better when the conversation is over.

A Shimmering Image From Childhood

Clover, come, let me comb your hair. Those were the words from Mama – three times she would call. At the third call, Clover was out of the house running down the road, crying like an owl. "I don't want my hair to be combed!" I ran to Mrs. Dor's house and under her bed crying. Then, whatever else Dor was doing, she would stop, take me into her lap and take her gentle time to comb through my thick hair. She combed more gently than my mama. Then I would fall asleep on Mrs. Dor's bed, until Mama came to get me. I love Mrs. Dor as a second Mom. Even when I got pregnant at 18, Mrs. Dor still went on caring for me.

Clover

Spring Acrostic Poem

S o, so cool, the leaves started sprouting

P ure fresh air and time for geese settling

R aising sun from the east is amazing

I n all days it seems so dazzling

N ight is feeling dark and free

G od is always ahead.

Once I Believed

Once I believed that everyone would live forever
Until I realized it is a never never
We are only visitors in this world
Men, women, boys and girls
Therefore we should all be loving and kind
And share with each other a peaceful mind.

Sometimes I Find Myself

Sometimes I find myself staring away not even realizing what is going on around me. Then my thoughts drift away. It seems as if I am on a different planet. Sometimes I try to block out everything. When will I come to reality? Oops, it's real! You are here. Come back, Clover, come back.

Clover

So, Here I Am

So here I am sitting in a Lifestories class. So far I'm enjoying myself. I finally have a chance to exhale, relax and write whatever comes to mind. I'm able to put the past day's events behind me and thank God for getting me this far. So here I am ready to write a chapter of the story of my life from beginning to end, also waiting to hear everyone else's words of their life that they express through pencil and paper.

Self Portrait Haiku

Who is this Celia?
she's a vision of beauty
Queen of her Castle

I Enter The Scene

From a calendar picture.

I enter the scene and don't know where I am. I see long strong green stems, too tall for me to see the top. Am I lost in the world of the giants? It seems like it, everything is so far away from me to the sky. Oh my, a rope drops from the top and fearlessly I climb the long stem. The sweet smell of floral fragrance starts to dance in my nose. As the wind blows the smell gets stronger, and as I continue to climb, the picture gets clearer. Oh wow! It's a flower bigger than life, the most beautiful I've ever seen. The dew on the petals are like pools of water as they fall from one petal to the next. I see myself sliding from petal to petal. As I enter the bud I hear the roar of a tiger. The flower opens up and facing me is the prettiest bunch of tiger lilies I've ever seen! They have orange petals with brown stripes, and little purple specks. I am sure this is nature's beauty in rare form!

Celia "Ciddy"

In The Quiet Room

In the quiet room there's silence, of a physical standpoint, but spiritually I hear the words that flow from my heart. Sorrow lives here no more, pain is gone, only the sounds of love, kindness and song. In a quiet room I can see all types of things: tranquility, serenity, peace, stillness. In a quiet room I can feel the music bouncing off the walls causing my heart to beat in unity with the bouncing…that only I can feel. My soul dances. I'm happy at last! in the quiet room.

Solitude

Breezy, cloudy, open, breath-taking is my area of solitude. Quiet, peaceful, wow!! I can exhale. My private hide-a-way that the whole compound can see. Solitude, a place to think, pray and cry, to laugh, sing praises and dance. A place of my own where I am free, free to be me. There's no right and wrong in Ciddy's place of solitude, just a far away place that is yet so near. Only I have the key to unlock my solitude. It's not lonely, it's where me and my mind can run free.

My Hands Haiku

I have lovely hands
my hands define who I am
I sit and watch them

At This Moment Now Haiku

At this moment now
I love how much I've grown
expression in ink

Celia "Ciddy"

140

It Was The Night Of The Full Moon

It was the night of the full moon and all the animals in the forest were celebrating. First, the fox, who was very clever, lit a huge bonfire in a clearing. Then the deer laid out a feast of roots and berries. The bears brought honey. The raccoons played tambourines, and everyone danced. The lions roared. The squirrels ran up and down the trees, giggling. The bobcats told stories passed down by the elders. The moon, oh the moon, she looked down from the heavens, casting beams of radiant light on the happy creatures who frolicked below, and when everyone was finally exhausted, they fell sound asleep and dreamed in unison.

When I Look In The Mirror I See

When I look in the mirror I see an old woman, a young woman, a child, an empress, a woman of all races and countries, a person who has lived before, many times, and who uses that wisdom to write her stories, to comfort others, to comfort herself.

When I look in the mirror I see silver hair, black hair, very short curly hair, very long thick hair, hair in braids, hair flowing down my back, the mane of a wild woman.

When I look in the mirror I see someone I am still learning to love, to understand, and to cherish. A person is an endless reservoir of selves, of personalities, of longings, accomplishments, memories, regrets and victories.

In the mirror I see every facet of my face and body, every wrinkle, sag, and blemish. In that same mirror I see a radiant goddess who is eternal, and splendid, spreading love and acceptance wherever she shines her light…

Katya

Leaf Haiku

Gold veins reach upwards
all through your body, brown leaf
I feel your life force

Shiny side, dull side
this leaf, like me, has her moods
all of life is mixed

In The Quiet Room

In the quiet room the women wrote. That was the amazing thing, that having a quiet place to think, feel and imagine made the pen and pencils move as if guided by magic. And indeed, the women found that their thoughts and emotions had a radiant glowing quality to them, as if the Spring sunlight had infiltrated their bodies, their consciousness.

One woman in particular was grateful for the quiet room. Here she could reflect on what mattered to her, without distraction. And she hoped the other women were striking gold, creating their own treasure, in the quiet room.

Katya

Cabin In The Woods

Students were guided through a visualization in which they discover an old trunk in a deserted cabin and open it to find... This is a good example of how each individual finds their own "treasure" when the opportunity arises for their imaginations to create it...

What I found in the old trunk in this cabin in the woods: I pull out some old but beautiful silk scarves, about six different colors. As I reach my hand back in, I feel something cold like steel. Wow, it's a whole band -- drums, guitars, keyboards, mics, and a couple of saxophones. Before I can put my hand back in, I hear voices saying, "Is she gonna help us out?" I look down in the trunk and there stand five of the prettiest women I've ever seen, and each one of them has on a dress that matches one of the six scarves. The loudmouth one says "Are you gonna help us out!?" Confused and surprised, I nodded yes! As I was pulling them out, they started harmonizing. As I helped the last one out, she pulls with her a beautiful dress that matches the sixth scarf. All of a sudden the dress was on me, the music started, and I realize that it's my band I lost fifteen years ago!

Celia "Ciddy"

A cabin in the woods with a light so bright. I step in, look around, on a search to find something strange, maybe even different. An ancient trunk sits in the corner by the bed. Inside my head I hear "There might even be a treasure." I lift the quilt with ease and grace and inside looks dark, so I stick my hand in and all I find is a hat and a church fan.

Lamisha

In the woods one day I walked into an empty cabin. There was only a beautiful cedar trunk. I looked in and found an unbelievable treasure of golden chalices, gold trimmed volumes of history books, crystal goblets and silk scarves. There was a letter in the trunk. It said that anyone who finds these treasures should take care of them and take them home.

Dahlia

Cabin In The Woods

A cabin in the woods caught my eyesight from a great distance.

I was walking through the woods and I saw the cabin made of just plain wood. It was very beautiful with a lot of white daisy flowers surrounding it, and between the daisies were yellow roses. The scent of the flowers was awesome! I peeked through the windows, the cabin was empty. All it had was an old trunk placed in the middle of the floor. It had no locks on it. I took my hands out of the pockets of my jacket, and opened the trunk, which squeaked. I reached in and there was a rose, and then a pink, yellow and white old blanket, very comfortable and cozy, and also some old pajamas. I immediately put them on, lay on the blanket, and fell asleep as if it had been given to me to have a big nap. I did not feel scared, I felt as if I were at home. In this cabin the thought of being alone was just bright and so was the light of the moon. The stars shone so beautifully from the window. I lay down and felt at peace. I shall never forget this day through to night – I lost track of time because of feeling so peaceful...

Berta

In the trunk I found gold of all kinds and ancient trinkets. Wait, look, it's a portrait! Maybe of the owner. Also a big brown envelope filled with papers and instructions. On one of the papers marked these words: "Dig under the third oak tree from the left of the cabin." The rest is my secret. I am so happy I walked in the woods and found that cabin. My whole life has been changed ever since.

Clover

Old Trunk Haiku

Dress for a princess
that fits me to perfection
fabric of white silk

Christina Star*

Cabin In The Woods

I was surprised to see a cabin in the middle of the forest. I peeked in the dusty windows to see that it was uninhabited, no sign anyone had lived there for a long time. The door was ajar and spiders had spun webs in the rafters. In the dark corner, only dimly illuminated, I saw an old cedar chest. Surprised, I pulled on the lid, and it creaked open. Nervously I glanced in, not knowing what if anything was stored there. An old tattered quilt lay on top. I reached to pick it up, and my hand touched a small picture frame. The glass was still intact. I gently blew the dust off of it. There was a young child in a white dress, probably a first communion photo, in sepia tones. At the bottom was the name *Alana*. I was shocked, as this is my own daughter's name! I stared at the photograph and my heart began to pound. There was her darling round face and rosebud lips, but on the back was written December 1887. One hundred years exactly before my child was born! I sat for a long time on the dusty floor until twilight made it difficult to see. I had to take this precious object home. Who could possibly solve this mystery?

Katya

Note: As with all assignments, I always do the exercises with my students. Besides the pleasure of amassing more writing—stories of my life or of my imagination, or a blend of both—I find that by each of us sharing aloud, we begin to inhabit a collective identity. No two classes are alike; they each create their own unique chemistry. I find that by deeply listening to my students I form an indelible portrait of each individual. As I collect and re-read these entries now, the faces of each woman (and in the early anthologies, each man) rise up, and their eyes meet mine. We created these unforgettable moments—with pen, paper and trust—despite the barbwire that surrounded us. I include my entries not as Katya the teacher, but as Katya the writer, with her own quirks, foibles, longings and fulfillments.

Reflections on the Writing Class

What did I get out of this class? Expression, heart-felt, peace, liberty, the ability to exhale. Openness. Freedom of speaking from the heart. I was able to be free on the inside!

Celia "Ciddy"

This class was very informative. I highly appreciated it. It allowed me to open up my heart, mind and soul, with a sense of non-judgementalness.

Lamisha

I loved this class. For expressing every thought and true moment I've lived in my life. No judgment, all was considered in every expectation of our stories. I learned that we all share different feelings but we are women of love, women in life, that we all have families and loved ones in our minds. Thank you, teacher, for coming to be here!

Berta

This class has been relaxing and enlightening. Katya is vibrant, and full of life. I enjoyed hearing the other ladies tell their stories and finding my own meaning in their love and life. I appreciate the fact that Katya comes on her own time to teach us and be with us.

Christina Star*

Thanks to all my students for sharing their stories and listening to mine. We all grow, becoming transformed by each other's openness and creativity. What an inspiration and two-way mirror.

Katya

IMAGINATIONS
UNCOVERED

The power of the mind through the pen brings

Freedom!

Writings of Women at FCI

Summer 2015

FCI: Summer 2015

I have chosen to include the Summer 2015 publication of Imaginations Uncovered *in its entirety, as opposed to previous anthologies that were composed of excerpts of student writing from the original publication. I wanted readers to be able to visualize the literary review that inmates actually hold in their hand at the end of a six-week class. Thus, this anthology includes the introductory note to reader, the dedication page, table of contents, and all the writing that appeared in the original anthology. (Students chose which pieces to include, because over six weeks we produced many more stories and poems than the ones printed here.) The cover art by Billi-Jo, both the drawing of the book and pen and the words written on the book, were her original creation.*

✐ Note to reader

This writers' anthology is the result of six sessions of meeting together, for an hour and a half each time, allowing the muse to guide us on a journey, seeking (and finding) the "wisdom of the pen."

We write from "seed phrases" – all of us together, and then we share. Two examples of seeds (as you shall see), are "A lonely time" or "A magic moment." We write prose and poetry (haiku and acrostics), fact and fancy; we write our memories and our hopes; we let down our barriers and reach deep within for the creativity waiting to express itself.

This is not a writing contest. All my students know "No one can write your story -- or poem – but you." We are here to evolve as writers, to share our stories, to open our hearts to our common humanity.

The process is alchemy. The words born here, in such a short space of time, are alive with meaning, with grace, and with humor. We invite you, the reader, to journey with us. As you turn the pages, perhaps your own stories will come to mind; perhaps you too will gain the benefits of our time together.

I believe we are all mirrors to one another, and yet unique human beings. Life is a mystery, and in this class, we are free to explore its many dimensions, each of us a teacher, each of us a student.

Katya Sabaroff Taylor

Summer 2015

COVER GRAPHIC by Billi-Jo

Thanks to Kathy LaRose and Beth Nichols for their support of this LifeStories course, and for others at FCI who escorted me to and from class.

We dedicate this anthology
to all people doing time
and for the stories
inside us,
waiting for expression

"There is a vitality, a life force, an energy, a quickening, which is translated through you...and because there is only one of you in all time, this expression is unique. And if you block it, it will never exist"

Martha Graham, modern dancer

Table of Contents

§ MELINDA §

Ten Things I Love To Do

1) I love to cuddle with my children.
2) I love to talk to my mama.
3) I love to know the correct answer, the more obscure the information, the better.
4) I love to read.
5) I love to cook for people I love.
6) I love to make others feel loved and special.
7) I love to make people laugh.

I Remember A Room (An Excerpt)

I remember a room where my husband and I stayed towards the end. The end of our run. The end of us. It was the spare room in the house of an older couple that fancied themselves hippies, but they were tweakers like us. The walls were covered in those black, fake velvet color-by-numbers pictures that you fill in with fluorescent markers. Bizarrely there was a black light on the windowsill that lit up nothing, because nothing in the room was glow in the dark. The closet was used for storage, but the dresser we could put our things in, though I didn't because it was too much work packing my belongings back up while I cried and told my husband I was DONE, and meant it this time, which was every other evening....

A Lonely Time

A lonely time in my life has been my incarceration. I am very far from home, so I very rarely see my family. My family is not great at sending mail, so I gave up running to mail call two years ago. I miss my family so much. I realize this must be how badly they missed me, when I was out there running the streets. I miss my children and am so filled with remorse and regret over everything I've missed and will miss before I get home. I miss my parents and am scared of losing my dad... I've realized I didn't have a friend in the world on the streets. That lifestyle changes

153

everything. Makes real friendships impossible. I'm lonely because what I did out there defined me. But I'm not that girl anymore. When I got locked up, I remember writing my husband and telling him I didn't know who I was, if I was not "Randy's wife." The lack of response told me I'd need to figure it out. My constant companion has been myself, and since I didn't like her very much, or even know her that well, I felt very lonely. I know who I started as, who I was, who I wanted to be, and who I will never be again. But who I am now? Not sure yet. But I think that when I can be back with my children and my family, I will remember what I'm made of. I won't feel lonely because I'll be where I belong.

A Magic Moment

A magic moment was staring into my daughter's unblinking eyes when they placed her in my arms for the first time. All at once in this infinite moment, time paused, nothing else mattered, and the meaning of my life was clear. I was put here so she could exist. Because all my shortcomings were meaningless in the face of her perfection.

Haiku

All these women's pain
poured onto paper at last
becomes beauty now

Self Portrait Haiku

No longer selfish
wounded, wiser, now awake
honest with myself

Loved so hard it hurt
lost myself along the way
finding my way back

Freedom Acrostic Poem

F inally letting go of all the things that have held me prisoner

R ealizing I was shackled long before I was arrested

E very person who told me I was worth nothing until I believed them

E very addiction that robbed me of what was beautiful

D eciding that I am more than my past, my regrets, my failures

O nly I can let myself out of this cage I've stayed locked in so long

M y past, my pain, is my story, but my future has yet to be written.

I Enter The Scene

I stand, the cool shade of the tree at my back, the bright sun warming my face. I look down at the waves beneath me, listening to the hiss and gentle moan of the surf against the rocks. The mist rises up, caresses my arms, my neck, my face. I lean in, listening to secrets it whispers to me....

My Life Is A Book Haiku

My life is a book
some chapters are sad, but there's
a plot twist you'll love

Rain Slipper – a Two Noun Story

It was time. He had finally fallen asleep, exhausted from his rage, lulled by the storm outside.

The storm inside had raged for hours. She wept now as she looked at her face in the mirror. Swollen, already purple, scraped bloody. It was time.

She quickly and quietly grabbed what she needed. Tucked the baby into her car seat, snugged her purse in next to her, and covered it all with a blanket so her baby girl would stay dry. Stuffed a backpack with formula, clothes, diapers, and a few essentials for herself.

It was time. Now while he was still dead to the world. No time for regrets. No time to mourn. No time for hesitation.

She pulled on her coat, then one of her boots, but when she tried to pull on the second one the pain was excruciating. Her ankle was already so swollen. She was certain he had broken it. Never mind. She settled for a slipper on that foot.

It was time. She gathered the bag and the baby up, and she only glanced back once. She quietly closed the door behind her. Stepping off the porch, her slipper-clad foot was immediately soaked in an ankle deep puddle, and freezing. But that was fine. Extreme cold will shock you awake. It was time.

❦ CHARLENE ❦

Ten Things I Love To Do

Watch a sunrise
Talk to my daughter
Eat chocolate
Read a good book
Go shopping
Feel a cool breeze on my face
Decorate a Christmas tree
Cook Thanksgiving dinner
Go swimming
Go fishing

Once Upon A Time – A Seed Story

Given phrases are in italics.

Once upon a time, a cute little rabbit was created in my mind. Sometimes, when *I close my eyes*, little creatures spring forth in my head like that. Then *stories flow out* of my mind about such a creature as the rabbit. I often wonder *what's in the silence* of others' minds – do they imagine cute little creatures, or do they conjure demons and monsters in their heads that consume them and drive them to destruction? People are like little imagined rabbits and demons and monsters – different as night and day. What do you see in your mind's eye when you close your eyes at night?

Haiku

Once upon a time
three sisters were together
now there are but two

At this moment now
these women are my sisters
with pencils in hand

Hands Haiku

My hand is like me
with a wrinkle here and there
strong hand, strong woman

When I Was A Child

When I was a child I used to hide from my Daddy every evening when he came home from work. Now don't misunderstand. I didn't do this because I was afraid of him. I did it because it was a silly little game that we played that made me giggle with delight each time I heard him ask my mother, "Honey, where is that young'un?" I am sure he already knew the answer to his question because I always hid in the same place, which was behind his favorite chair.

One of my safest, happiest memories of when I was a child is when Daddy "found" me and lifted me in his arms and held me there, tight against his chest.

Rain Slipper – A Two Noun Story

The girl in the blue pleasant blouse looked at me and smiled a big, toothy grin. "Hi," she gushed a little too loudly for my liking. "How are you?" Her drawl was definitely Southern. She looked like a hippie with her long braid and flowing colorful skirt.

"My name is Kita," she continued. "Do *you* think it's going to rain?"

I put down the book I was reading. So much for solitude I thought dryly. I had gone to the park to enjoy the cool, brisk morning by myself, without company.

As I eyed Kita's feet, I answered, not too kindly, "Well the weatherman predicted 90% rain, but you know how it is. They are never right."

She saw me looking at her shoes and looked embarrassed. "They were my mother's," she explained quietly "She died of cancer four years ago, when I was thirteen. I wear them every year on the anniversary of her death. She was a ballet teacher and the most beautiful ballerina on earth."

She smiled then, and it melted my heart. "The slippers are beautiful," I told her. "I love satin, and baby blue is my favorite color."

She smiled again and said "Well I have to go. I hope you have a great day." Before I could respond, she was gone.

That lovely wispy girl touched my heart that day, and I always think of her and her mother on the anniversary of our meeting in the park, before the rain came.

My Life Is A Book Haiku

My life is a book
to be read to learn the truth
about who I am

Guided Visualization: Cabin In The Woods

One day I walked through a meadow of tall green grass, sweet smelling and soft under my bare feet. I heard birds singing overhead as I felt the soft breeze on my face. I went further across the meadow toward a grove of trees – hardwoods, mostly, but a few tall pines were there too, and their lost needles softly scratched my feet as I walked across them. There was a path through the trees, and I followed it, until I came to a cabin in a clearing.

The cabin was abandoned, and I couldn't resist its temptation. I pushed on the door and it creaked open. There, in the corner of the single room stood an old trunk that looked like it should have belonged to my great grandmother. Carefully I eased the top open to see what was inside. It was at that moment that I got the shock of my life! Huddled in the corner sat a little leprechaun with a long beard and wearing a pointy red hat and dark blue overalls.

"What are you doing, you meddlesome woman?" he demanded. "This is my hiding place and you have found me. Now I must find another place to live and hide and it's all your fault! Blagh!"

Before I even had time to get over my shock and respond to him, he jumped out of the trunk and ran out the door, shaking his head and muttering under his breath. I don't know what became of him, but I do know now that leprechauns really do exist.

At This Very Moment

At this very moment, I am thinking about teaching and learning. I am thinking about what fun I used to have teaching my son and daughter to make cookies, and how cute they were, standing on stools with aprons on and rolling pins in hand, and with more flour on their faces than on their floured surface...

❧ SUSANNA ❧

At This Very Moment

At this very moment I am embarking on a journey beyond pressure points and controlled thoughts into free soul movement. I whisper through yesterdays in my mind and leave it behind, dusty – no longer displayed in my being. Who I was is not who I am going to be. Tomorrow holds the promise of my focus, my determination and growth. At this very moment, I am alive – glittering in the aura of purpose – redefining who I am and proud to be who she is.

Soup Husband – A Two Noun Story

I fell in love with a canned soup. Believe me, I did. Alphabet soup to be exact. Made up of all X's and O's and that delicious taboo beef flavoring. Maybe it was because I'd never seen a man, created out of soup. But it was planet Pluton and the strangest things seemed normal. You could look up on any given day and see a rainbow of sneakers drifting across the purple sky. They say the sky was purple there because a blue bullfrog loved grapes soooo much that when he burped from his full, fat tummy, he covered the once gray sky in his favorite flavor. Maybe I liked my husband so much since I gave up red meat and the smell of him brought up memories of thick, rich beef steak. Maybe that's why, on the cold wintry day, on planet Pluton, when the sky snowed popcorn flavored jellybeans, I ate him.

A Lonely Time

A lonely time is when you're laid out in your destiny, giving birth to that dream inside you. The dream that has been festering in your womb, growing steadily, like the rhythmic drumming off the salty shores of Cuba... That dream is all you had in that lonely time. When you are in an overcrowded space - but your stomach is the only one rumbling. Your soul knocking on your anxiety, whispering – not here, this isn't your place. You look upward, simply because everyone else just looks in front of themselves and ahead just isn't enough. Lateral movement can't account for the pain. It's lonely, laid on your back, when you were just on your feet. Now you're in agony, your guts being torn from the belly of protection. You gasp in unsurety as your bowels twist themselves in knotty figure 8's. No one can hold your hand in reassurance because they don't rightly know where you're going. All of you is alien to their mediocrity. So you gap your legs wide – blood oozing from your pores where the sweat should be. Tears fall in the shape of question marks onto the lonely road called remarkable.

You scream out with the force of a tribe of women watching their men, children being sold into the unknown. The anguish of it all thunders across the universe, tearing holes in the seams... the searing, hot pain bears down on you like Satan does the just. You wrap the loneliness up, grab hold with two hands and you push that thing that's been inside of you out, with all the truth you have in you, because all you know is what you tell yourself. In that loneliest moment, when that thing is being birthed from within, when all things in life align, and purpose comes with undoubtable, defined clarity, in all it's glory, you see your dream before you – whole and defined – in 3D – you know you'll never be lonely again, because you have the joy of perseverance as your lifelong companion.

Acrostic Name Poem

S ophisticated challenge wrapped in beauty

U ndulating hips moving to Afro Cuban drum beats

S eeing beyond the edges and corners of the world's box

A nticipating the next wonder revealed

N eeding to freely ride my own roller coaster of thought
and emotion

N ever expecting to fail

A live

Haiku

Wondrous in hope

perseverance moves my hand

I awake a whole

At this moment now

I am no longer afraid

to bare my soft heart

I Love To

I love to run. I leave the notes of sorrow behind that play in my ears. I run towards my future – a destiny untethered to the place in which I stand. I feel my breath pushing through me, the force of my soul expanding, becoming greater than any circumstance. With every beat of my foot into the grassy hill, I scream in my mind "I give it back." All of the negative energy, the sadness, the anger, I give back to the earth and in return I receive self-forgiveness and unmerited, merciful peace.

Leaf Haiku

Veined in creation
blistered from the summer sun
leaf, my soul in soil

Lifting from formica
running in a way I can't
leaf, amazing, free

I Remember A Room

I remember a room filled with fluttering dragons wings and butterflies born of fire. A phoenix perched, in all its glory, on the highest arch of the trestlewood ceiling, raining tears of toasted cinnamony ashes, healing the warrior's wounds – he who carried my guarded, precious heart, wrapped in royal purple velvet. In this room he stood tall, strong and magnificently proud of the scars that draped across his body like early morning sunshine speaking its first hellos to the world. In this room, with every beat, my heart echoed his name – shouting it across the infinities. In this room, filled with creatures and man – who unsheathed sword and claw in my honor -- in this room, I was home.

Haiku

At this moment now

writing flushes out secrets

mirrored is my mind

My life is a book

do you think you can read me

escape in my dreams

Guided Visualization ~ Cabin In The Woods

I walk through the meadow, awed at the sound of peace. I stop, breathing in the air from the south side of the wire, marveling at freedom. My shoes feel damp from the early morning dew, leaves crunch under the soles as I walk along the narrow path before me. Looking up, I see an old, rustic cabin, something that I would imagine to be lifted from historical fiction pages. Hmm, I wonder. Does anyone live there? Tentatively I push the rusty door open with shouts of "Hello?" The echo of my own singsong question is the only response I hear. On pointed tippy toes I glide slowly over the inch-thick crusty floor. It feels like maple syrup and dirt have fossilized into an almost natural linoleum

Through the mist of dust bunnies shimmering on light that seeps through the spotted windows, I notice an ancient trunk in the far off corner. History maybe? Supplies from a long ago war? A body even, mummified, picked clean by strange bugs? I carefully, and not the least bit afraid, lift the trunk's lid. Banging it against the cabin wall, surprised by the weight of it, I jump. Breathing in slowly, to settle my nerves, I look down to see a beautiful, creamy, yellow chiffon scarf. I wrap my fingers in the softness, tugging at it lightly. As it slides free from the confines of darkness my nose is assaulted by the scent of lilacs. Lilacs and laughter? I scramble backwards, racing against my heartbeat for the win. What the hell is that??? My mind frantically searches for a spoon, a fork, a lid, anything to fend off.... the red, purple and blue fairies that are suspended in mid air, flapping boysenberry dust from their wings – giggling into the fresh morning air.

♪ VICTORIA ♪

At This Very Moment

At this very moment, I'm beginning to relax. My mind and my spirit feel very connected to this room, the light that is contained in it, and the pencils scribbling across the other pages in the room. I'm not sure what to expect but somehow that's okay. I'm learning to accept these things as they come, more and more as I continue to grow in my life. So knowing all the answers isn't what is paramount anymore. I almost feel like a leaf or a flower in the breeze. It's very Zen...

Once Upon A Time – A Seed Story

Given phrases are in italics.

Once upon a time, there was a land that was open and had rolling plains with tsimpsilas, or wild turnips and onions, that I used to help my aunt dig up. *I close my eyes* and I'm there with my little stick trying to dig down deep enough so as not to break the stalk and root of the tell-tale flower.

Those memories, those instances of "once upon a time" are like trying to gather all the pages from a lost, torn, damaged book. Where are all the pages? I don't know. Perhaps that's why telling the story, the actual oral tradition, is so important to me. When I start talking and remembering the *stories flow out*. Sometimes I can talk for hours, just remembering.

I miss my reservation. I miss those moments on the top of those small hills on my family's land. It's quiet there with only a breeze.

Now, imagining I'm there, *"What's in the silence?"* I ask myself. Only me.

At This Moment Now Haiku

At this moment now
I am sated, feeling fresh
fed and washed with words

166

Cast of Characters

I am an old woman, already working on 90 years or so I think. I don't know, it seems counting became less and less important over the years. They don't want me upstairs and they don't want me downstairs, so here I am still. I like to wake up around four in the morning to get my first cup of coffee and sit in the pre-dawn light quietly, and so I can hear the gentle snores of my grandchildren.

I see sometimes things they don't see, so I keep these things to myself. I don't want to scare my sons or daughters. They might think I'm crazy or getting ready to make the journey, you know. I'm not. I'm just in a moment in my life where I have become like a child again...

Self Portrait Haiku

Proud stoic woman
cultured, silently searching
for wisdom's bright path

Name Acrostic

V aliant lover of learning

I nsightful, giving from the source within

C onnecting with all creation

T hrough speaking and touching and praying

O ver my loved ones like the Blessed Virgin

R otating them through my mind like a slide show

I n each breath is a prayer

A rduously keeping pace with the heart.

I Remember A Room

I remember a room. It was all concrete and steel with one sliver of a window about six inches wide. The whole world existed in those six inches. What I mean to say is that for me those six inches and the view it contained *was* the whole world. It may sound strange to say, tragic in fact, but I felt safe being cloistered away in that cell. Perhaps it was because it was a lonely time and I prayed all the time and talked to my unborn child, Josiah. Those were the last moments I had any type of physical closeness with any of my beloved children.

I recall reading so many times about how one could view incarceration as one might being in a monastery. And without knowing at that moment, maybe I was seeking out these types of reading materials, about monasteries or abbeys. So that room during my stay there in Pennington County became a sanctuary. Almost like a chapel. And when the sun would begin its descent into the horizon I would look out that window.

One evening I decided to write about what I was seeing out of that window. I was so bored and wanting to put my mind to work during the final lockdown after supper. I sat at the steel desk with its steel stool with paper and pencil in hand and waited. My roommate was quietly reading the newspaper, lost in her own pursuits.

Suddenly as if by some miracle or what you might call a magic moment, I saw a deer come over the hill from between the houses in the distance. It was foraging and making its way through the neighborhood. It must have been really quiet that evening because it was eating at a leisurely pace.

Then I noticed another deer, this one with a fawn. And then another and another. Slowly it dawned on me that there was a whole herd of these does with their young. I must have been very focused and interested in observing what that first deer was doing because I really didn't realize how many there were until I blinked a few times and the other white tails could be perceived by my mind.

It was incredible. They stayed that way for about ten minutes, just taking an evening stroll like families sometimes do. They seemed so peaceful. I was so excited but I didn't dare move or say anything to my bunkie, for fear I might miss something. I knew I was witnessing something that at that very moment perhaps no one else in the world was.

I turned to tell my bunkie and it's like they heard me and the noise of her paper moving, but no that's not possible, is it? Anyway, she looked to see but alas they were already making bounds over the hilltop into the cover of the shadows on the other side.

Far Into My Future

Far into my future, I see a woman whose face is lined and wrinkled, like the terrain of the Badlands in South Dakota. Who has two little braids decorated with silver and a little housedress. No one wears simple dresses like that except old ladies.

She remembers a time when she heard and read the stories about her people. She remembers and tells those stories to her grandchildren, because that's what grandmothers do. And they make bread. Bread and wakalyapi.

Old grandmother has a little squat house down in a ravine, close to a spring because that's where the best water is. That's also where those really ancient little Indians live, close by the springs. They call them wiwila's. When she was younger, probably all the way up until her 30's, she was afraid to see one. Not now. Old people have seen so much that it's really hard to scare them.

Little grandmother has stories socked away in chests, in cabinets, on shelves, in coin purses. In places even she's forgotten. One day when she's gone, her children and her grandchildren will come for her belongings. Will they know every story that is contained in those old useless things before they burn them? Only the ones who listened...

MAHLONA

An Ideal Day (An Excerpt)

I awake to the feel of your lips raining kisses all over my face, and the sound of your voice telling me to wake up and play with you. Without opening my eyes I ask you in a deep sleep-thickened voice "What time is it?" "It's one pm," you reply. At hearing this I moan and try to roll over and snuggle down into the blankets. At which point you snatch the covers off and I whimper, knowing what's coming next -- I will be putty in your hands, and my sleep is over. I feel the bed shift as you reach for something on the nightstand, I hear the flick of a lighter. The bed shifts again as you sit up and a heartbeat later I feel something against my bottom lip in a silent command to open my mouth. I part my lips and you slide a cigar between them. As I take a pull on it I get the taste of Goodtimes Fruit Punch. I feel your body against mine as you lean in to kiss my neck, I lay there puffing on my cigar as you work to make me your willing slave.

An hour later after I have begged, screamed and moaned for mercy, you tell me "go take a shower and get dressed." All I can manage is an mmm hmmm as I get up from the bed and hope I can make it to the bathroom without my knees giving out on me. I make it, turn the water on full blast, step in and let our multi-head shower beat down on me. I finish my shower and grab my towel off the rack. As I'm toweling off, I look at the sink and find a steaming mug of coffee. Halting in my drying process, I grab the coffee and look down and see another cigar waiting for me in the ashtray. I take a cautious sip of the coffee and moan at the taste of pure nirvana. As I set the coffee down and pick up the cigar, I think "That woman has definitely ruined it for anyone else. I ain't going no damn where." I light my cigar and finish getting dressed....

Freedom Acrostic

F ighting for a chance to shine

R eaping the rewards of sacrifice

E xtinguishing all doubt of your greatness

E scaping from a self imposed imprisonment of the mind

D aring to dream of greatness

O bliteration of all obstacles placed in my way

M arching forward head up, shoulders back, to make my mark on the world

Far Into My Future I See...

"You are destined for greatness!" I can probably count on one hand how many times I've heard this in my life as opposed to the countless times I was told, "You will never amount to anything. You're worthless, dumb, lazy, lack commitment. All around lacking."

It's funny what you will believe if you hear it enough. The power that can have over you has the potential to leave you crippled mentally, leave you searching for approval and acceptance in the damndest places. Worse yet, they leave you shackled and imprisoned – mind, body and soul.

Today I make my stand and say *no more*!! No more seeking the love and approval of others, wanting them to, no, *needing* them to believe and have faith in me. I'll do it for myself. I approve of me, believe in me, and most of all, love me. Not so far into my future I see the greatness I'm destined for.

I Remember A Room

As a young adult I walked around laughing at life, doing as I pleased with no remorse for the turmoil I may have caused in other people's lives. Now here I sit, in the back end of my 30's with serious regrets on how I've allowed, as if I had a choice, my life to unfold. I try to figure out what went so horribly wrong. Then I remember a room. With a man sitting up high that deemed me unworthy of my freedom and told me "I now sentence you to 211 months in federal prison."

My mind is scrambling to do the math as I figure 211 = 17 years and 7 months, my heart stops, my knees buckle, and my mind screams "That's not right!! It can't be!!" In the next instant my heart resumes its beat and my knees snap to attention. "My mother won't be there when I get home!"

In that moment nothing else mattered but her, my mind was forcing me to think of someone else because at that moment had I thought of me, I would have literally gone insane. But why? I didn't value the life I had anyway. I was out there thumbing my nose at fate on a daily basis, and now I sit, at the end of my 17 year journey with my travel plans in hand, wishing I could go back and change so many things as I remember a room...

A Magic Moment

What is a magic moment? Well, that depends on who you ask. To a baseball fan, it's when bases are loaded, it's the bottom of the 9th and the home team is down by 3 and the batter at the plate swings at the first pitch and smashes a game-winning, walk-off grand slam. To a music lover, it's the height of a crashing crescendo in their favorite song. To an artist it's the final stroke in a masterpiece that their muse deserted them on. To happy parents, it's the sound of the first cry of a newborn baby.

To me a magic moment was when I kissed the woman I want to spend the rest of my life with for the first time. It was more than a meeting of lips. (Yes, to some I know this will sound corny as hell!) I felt my world shift on its axis. I knew my life would never be the same.

I'd finally understood what the songs, books, and movies were talking about when they said the word "Love."

Oh, but they lied. It's not easy and it's not always the best feeling in the world. But thinking of the song she puts in my heart when she says "I love you", feeling the sun shine on me when she smiles my way, or the feel of her lips on mine, reminds me of that very first magic moment...

Hands Haiku

Enough harm is done
we need gentleness and peace
feel my hands caress

Hands moving swiftly
as my masterpiece unfolds
got to get this right

Hands torn and ragged
telling me their tragedy
wow, what a story

STEPHANIE

I Love To

I love to feel the sunshine on my skin. The warmth of the sun radiating down upon me lets me know a sense of freedom not all can experience. A gentle breeze sweeps past me and tickles the very hairs on my arms. I close my eyes to dream of my favorite place and hear the ocean as it whispers against the shores of the Gulf Coast. Envisioning the aquamarine reflection and feeling the sand between my toes gives me a peace like none other. Tranquility floods my inner soul and just being able to step out of the physical location that keeps me bound for a brief moment is pure delight. My heart finds joy in taking in the earth's radiance and energy as it fuels my body and rejuvenates me with the power to keep going. A temporary escape into my vision, before reality sets in, it's just me and my sunshine moment, as it warms my skin and lightens my heart.

A Magic Moment

As I envelop myself in thoughts of the past, I linger on memories that hold a greater significance to my soul. Such as the beauty of a magic moment that causes my heart to race, my cheeks to flush and my feet to float on nothing but air. Pushing myself out of this current reality, a lonely time, I envision what my future will become when I am able to fly like a bird again, cage-free and soaring through life, no shackles, no chains, no boundaries, no reins.

An overwhelming sense of peace floods my soul because although physically I may be bound, spiritually I am free. Escaping and moving along to the next thought I close my eyes and remember a room, a place of safety where I could close out the world and be who I wanted to be through a piece of paper and my favorite pen. An act of expression of who I am and a flow of creativity as I silently pour out and secretly share my heart, mind and soul.

Closing my thoughts as they come to an end, I open my eyes and a deep sigh washes over me. Until my next adventure and escape I endlessly seek ways to maintain my freedom despite the restrictions set before me...

Far Into The Future

Far into my future I see a life well-lived, full of purpose and overflowing with love. I want to sit back with my family and reminisce on times past. Silly moments, great achievements, and even the struggles that made us who we are. Side by side with my best friend and the man I love, we'll discuss even then what our future will hold. We'll sit and converse about the unique qualities and differences in each one of our children, and how the paths they chose to take on their own led them to where they are in that current season. Remembering loved ones long gone, and thumbing through albums and heirlooms as we rock side by side on the veranda of our beach house retirement home.

Far into the future I see us full of youth, active and ready to continue our journey as the years go by, only ripening with age like a fine wine. Day by day as the love we share grows, and as iron sharpens iron, so shall we keep one another strong and vibrant as the moments we cherish turn into the very future we planned so long ago.

Once Upon A Time – A Seed Story

Given phrases are in italics.

Once upon a time, a young woman by the name of Destiny grew up in a home where all seemed well to outer appearances. Destiny loved to write and for the most part she struggled with the inner turmoil of a frustrating home-life, despite what it looked like on the outside. Most of the time she would allow the *stories to flow out;* other times there would be nothing. The escape to her pain would be the expression she could use with her words. It wasn't the moments when she was with others that made her happy, it was the comfort and solace of her writing that was *in the silence.* Sometimes she would dream of a fairy tale life, and was hopeful of better days, as she would say if *I close my eyes* the sadness will just go away.

Destiny was not aware that she would continue to search and long for a love she so desired but was never able to experience. Until one day many years passed and someone would enter her life that would turn it all around. A light came on inside of her and because of the lengthy struggle, for a time her writing stopped. However, in the midst of passion and love the words began to flow, and the flame was ignited once more.

Hands Haiku

Replica of mom's
our hands are one and the same
yet unique in prints

Self Portrait Haiku

Strength, courage, wisdom
a woman of great morale
my future is bright

A Moment In Time (Excerpts)

Two hearts beating in one accord. A moment in time so magical nothing can compare to the fate that awaited our arrival. Never anticipating the time constraints or circumstances that causes us to reach the destination of our collision. How we came to be was only by happenstance. Deeper levels of intimacy on a spiritual plane consolidating our union without physical interaction ever taking place... Submerged in the adoration of our exploration into one another's individuality, we start this journey together... A desire to be enraptured in the enchantment and sweet tender moments with you alone, I anticipate the exhilaration and breathtaking excursions we'll take pleasure in as we discover each other though the years ahead. Conscious of our profound connection and amazed at how deep the communication between us has become. Floating on hope, walking in faith, trusting in our love until the day we are united as one.

One Of Life's Great Pleasures – An Excerpt

One of life's greatest pleasures is opening my mind to thoughts, feelings and emotions that have been suppressed for so long. A sense of freedom washes over me. Despite my current circumstances, I've stepped into a sphere of independence like I've never experienced. Eyes wide open, motivated in pursuit of opportunity at my very disposal, I can't turn around and allow my past to chain me and keep me bound. Being in a state of oppression for so long, one's foresight on life can severely diminish. Breaking out of this mentality to regain the victory that slipped from my grasp so long ago, I'm ready to conquer life and all it has to bestow upon me. I can finally dream again. I want to see the world with a different set of eyes. No longer dimmed from the gravity of the ache that so heavily obstructed my view, the windows to my soul are a sparkling radiant illumination that glimmers. Heading into this new chapter, achieving greater success, obtaining previously unreachable goals, and like never before, shooting straight for the stars.

My Life Is A Book Haiku

My life is a book
torn pages, broken margins
restored once again

ৡ PEPPA ৡ

Once Upon A Time – A Seed Story

Once upon a time there was a gallant knight. She was strong and tough and beautiful. She was a dog, with lots of yard to patrol. Every morning she goes out, with her neck twisted up to look to the tops of trees. She's proud and quick and very smart, but for some reason that day – there were no squirrels to hunt? - she decides to nap. She thinks if *I close my eyes* and wake up, maybe I'll find some birds or rabbits to chase.

With her eyes closed tight, the *stories flow out* of her puppy dog mind. She has lots to hunt. She sees a fox with a bright red tail, a few bugs, and birds with songs for her singing. She loves the sound but it's *what's in the silence* that will suit this hound.

Finally, she wakes, looking around the yard with her head held high, patrolling along. Out comes her gallant knight friends, the other three dogs. Soon there isn't even a bird with a song. Maggie gives up her armor and decides to play like a dog. They run and chase each other the rest of the day.

Leaf Haiku

The leaf's veins of life
from light to dark, small to big
when rain washes in

Perseverance blooms
in far away sad rooms
life's gloom left behind

178

A Shimmering Image

When love rode in like a gallant shining white horse with a prince and saved me from my self.

Unfailing, unconditional, undying love. Warm, comforting, companionate love.

The horses name is Hope, the Prince Perseverance.

They give me strength. I feel proud and tall with my head held high.

 No more does my heart cry.

Friendship And Beauty – A Two Noun Story

Friendship and Beauty were two trees in a field. One was a big oak with huge limbs and beautiful green leaves. The other was a maple tree just as big, with the same beautiful leaves and large brown limbs.

One day it was cold, with a strong north wind, that just about tore through the maple, and broke all its branches. Its poor leaves were falling rapidly. It was bare at the end.

The maple was crying, and cold, all the way to her bark. She was worried this was her end.

Just then, she felt a break from that horrible wind, as she was covered with the huge leaves from the oak tree, her old friend.

Name Acrostic

P assionate about life and love

E nthusiastic about faith and freedom

P ersevering through my time and troubles

P eaceful when full of thoughts about my family

A damant that my dog Maggie is the most beautiful in the world.

Guided Visualization – The Cabin In The Woods

I walk through the meadow, through the clearing, to the old cabin. The door creaks as it opens and I see an old wooden trunk. As I open it, there are lots of beautiful bright colors. A sundress, a soft light pink sundress. It slides on perfectly.

As I walk back out to the meadow, the breeze blows the soft material and it kisses my skin. The sun shines, giving me and all the flowers in the meadow light and life.

Free and beautiful I feel in my new dress. I walk slowly around the meadow, which is a canvas, one of God's most beautiful works of art. I feel whole and full, and my heart sings for joy, that I get to be a part of it all.

My new lovely pink dress fits in perfectly with the flowers in the meadow. They all smile up at me from a carpet of green grass. The birds sing, the bees fly, making life a very precious and wonderful sight to my tired and sad eyes.

Far Into The Future

I see life, I see me graduating in a beautiful blue robe. I see happiness and love, kindness and uncompromising faith. I see self-control, gentleness, effectiveness, peace, and lots of fun. I see my son and granddaughter in blue robes also, smiles and joy, laughter and security.

A Magic Moment

A magic moment in my dreams is the day that I'm home, on my porch, enjoying the breeze.

Watching my furry children run and play, chasing each other and scaring the squirrels away.

Holding my amazing man, with his blazing green eyes, feeling loved and comforted and satisfied.

Hugging my parents, making sure they know I'll never come back to this place.

Seeing myself, with my head held high, persevering through life with a huge sunshine in my sky, not sad or distraught, not listening to any more of the devil's lies.

My Life Is A Book Haiku

My life is a book
full of many ups and downs
of all, I'm author

⸱ BILLI-JO ⸱

I Remember A Room

I remember a room. It was a gloomy, dingy, dark and lonely room. I waited there trembling with fear. I was cold and wet from showering in front of four other women. With eyes staring and searching our bodies as we washed, the prostitutes were sprayed with a special chemical. Naked and afraid. What would happen to me in this place?

Dressed in bright orange, we walked in a straight line behind one another. My arms were filled with a thin, worn mat that would become my bed, a smelly, stained sheet, a blanket with holes throughout and a uniform with graffiti written all over it.

"Look straight, don't make eye contact!" he yelled. When someone passed he screamed "Stop and face the wall!" It was like a maze of concrete. I was the last one. Finally we arrived. I heard slamming of doors, cries of women and an officer cursing at them to shut up. I was escorted to the second level. We stopped at the second door. It popped open electronically as he pointed, "Get in!"

I hurried in, careful not to upset him, and rushed to the empty bed. There was a woman sitting alone. I tried not to look at her. Who was she? Will I be safe? It was cold. So cold I could see my breath in the air. Cold enough that I wondered if I might freeze to death in my sleep. Sleep. Yes, I needed sleep. Please God, let me sleep. Then maybe I would die. At least all of this would be over. Without my children I felt dead anyway. I wanted to die.

I lay there thinking of ways I could get to heaven – I could stop eating and drinking. Yes, that would do it. How long can someone survive without water? I prayed that night to Jesus. I was shaking. How could anyone live through this? I wondered. My heart was broken. Help me... Help me...I'm so cold.

It began at my toes. A warmth that moved up slowly throughout my body. At first I wasn't sure it was real, but it was. I felt a touch on my shoulder as I lay there stiff on my mat. When I turned I saw no one. I leaned over to peek at my bunkie, but she was asleep.

As I turned to face the wall again, I was instantaneously consumed with peace and a sense of love. In a room full of sorrow and hopelessness, I experienced comfort and strength. I'll never forget that room. The room where, for the first time in my life, I truly knew I wasn't alone, and would never be.

Hands Haiku

Amazing my hands
created to touch, feel, hold
to work, to live, to love

Freedom Acrostic

F ulfilling life's dreams wherever you are

R ecreating your future

E ntering the world of writing

E xperiencing life through the mind

D ancing under the stars

O pening your heart

M editating on God's word, living according to His purpose.

At This Moment Now Haiku

At this moment now
I'm filled with encouragement
wise minds surround me

I Enter The Scene

I enter the scene, oh how beautiful. The cool air, the smell of the trees, bring me peace. I walk through the bushes of yellow, then red, until I reach the rocks. What a glorious and magnificent creation. Just beyond I find a river with crystal clear water.

I sit to appreciate the natural wild, when I notice a large black bear in the water. It's fishing for trout. I watch as he paws through the water, slipping up is a shiny rainbow trout trying to escape. I am amazed to witness such a sight. The bear tries and tries until he finally succeeds. I'm breathtaken at his strength and beauty.

I need to move on, if I want to get to the top of the mountain that lies ahead. They say the view opens farther than the eye can see. I leave the bear behind, beginning my climb, with great anticipation for what lies ahead.

Haiku Moments

At this moment now
joy and heartache fill the room
life's journeys expressed

My life is a book
joy and pain fill the pages
love and loss inside

A mother away
still, my heart is home
waiting to return

A Guided Visualization – The Cabin In The Woods

I walk through the meadow. It is inviting with the songs of the birds and the rays of sunlight peeking through the trees. I follow the small path on the left, which leads me to an open field. There I see a cabin. "Who could live here?" I wonder. "It looks abandoned."

I push the door gently and it opens. "Hello – is anyone here?" I call.

I enter the cabin. It is definitely abandoned. There are cobwebs everywhere and you can hardly see out the windows. As I explore, I notice an old chest. I dust it off and open the lid. Something is wrapped up, being protected. "It must be something special. What could it be?"

I reach in and lift it out. Wrapped in cloth and string, I untie it. I am astonished at what I find. It appears to be some sort of scroll, written in another language, on paper I have never seen before. Could it be...? No, surely they aren't old Biblical scrolls!

The writing looks like Greek or Hebrew, but I can't tell for sure. I quickly and carefully wrap the scrolls up again and put them into my backpack. Eager to get back to town, my heart is racing with excitement! I must get back so I can begin my search for a theologian who can help me.

Three weeks later, we meet. I patiently but anxiously wait as he examines the findings. He looks up from his glasses and smiles....

❦ SOPHIE ❦

Ten Things I Love To Do

1. Be with my family. 2. Eat! 3. Sleep late. 4. Drink coffee.

5. Stay busy.

6. Read. 7. Listen to live music. 8. Learn new things.

9. Exercise. 10. Cuddle.

I Remember A Room

I remember a room where the pangs of heartache were felt for the first time. His bedroom, my safe-haven and all-important space. I remember the intensity of three years spent in and out of that same room. The beginning in which innocence was lost. The first time for everything. Habits were formed there. Addictions began there.

It was a plain white room, with a plush carpet, plain wooden dresser, and a box-spring mattress. It smelled like Cool Water cologne, weed smoke, and scented candles.

I remember that room. The endless hours spent there. Laughing, loving, and fighting. Mostly fighting. Never understanding each other because we were still too young to understand ourselves. Back and forth the cycle continued, but ultimately broke down.

That night I'll never forget, sitting on his bed for the last time. Both of us exhausted. Trying to make sense of our seemingly impossible 16-year-old lives. To assign some type of immortal significance to the emotions we felt in that moment.

Intensified further only by the lyrics coming through his stereo and the drugs coursing through our bodies. "No one will ever understand us," we agreed.

But ten years later, I can look back at that room and that moment. I look back at myself and it all makes sense. A teenage love deteriorated over time. Consumed by itself and then dissolved....

Hands Haiku

Like my grandmother's
long, slender and delicate
I never knew her

If my hands could choose
they would stay here all day long
intertwined with yours

A Precious Object

My precious object is my journal. This object is equal to my freedom and my friend. It is precious because within it I can find comfort, I can find solace.

It is my escape and retains my deepest thoughts, feelings and memories.

It is unconditional. I can turn to it for anything at any time. It serves many purposes.

I vent through it, I organize with it, I tell stories to it, I learn from it.

It is a typical composition notebook, black and white, bound with string and tape. Plastered with pictures and quotes I enjoy looking at. It is anything but typical to me.

It keeps my secrets and knows my weaknesses. I give to it and it gives back.

It holds the promise of memories kept, and it is my source of peace, as with all that came before it. And there have been many more before it.

My journal is my precious object because it is my second home. The writer inside me lives inside it.

Freedom Acrostic

F or the longest time I took it for granted

R ushing through life with no self-regard

E very day I miss it now but have to remember

E ven if they won't let me out

D on't lose sight of that which they cannot confine

O xygen, sunlight, dreams, and hope

M ust be that freedom is only a state of mind

Haiku Moments

At this moment now
my lungs breathe out and then in
I rest – my heart beats

Alive and thankful
exhausted but determined
ready for what's next

My life is a book
I can't stop turning pages
learning from each one

Guided Visualization – Cabin In The Woods

I walk through the meadow, wildflowers at my feet. I walk on and find myself on a path, a forest up ahead. The dense brush looks intriguing to me, and so I follow this path and walk on towards the tree line. The light changes as I enter the forest. Sunbeams streak down and dance at my feet. I walk across the soft moss-covered ground. The earth smells rich with dirt and plant life. The smell is fresh and comforting.

A cabin is up ahead and I go inside. There's an abandoned, forgotten feel to it. The cobwebs and dust have accumulated in every corner and surface. An old trunk catches my eye, and I don't hesitate to see what's inside. I'm eager to discover any clue as to this cabin's last inhabitants.

Inside I find an old quilt. It is large and worn, smelling of mothballs but still soft. It is hand sewn with perfect stitches. Squares of fabric both small and large are joined together to create this beautiful tapestry.

I sit on the floor of the old cabin, quilt in my arms, and ponder its maker. How long has it been in this trunk, untouched, unused. I imagine its owner curling up underneath it, draping it across her sleeping children, wrapping herself in it as she sits in front of the old wood burning stove.

I've found a treasure, I think to myself. A memory long forgotten. I smile and place the folded object back in the trunk. I feel at peace with my findings, but leave it there where I found it. Then I walk back through the woods towards the wildflowers...

§ KATYA §

At This Very Moment

At this very moment... a new class begins. The women pick up their pencils and the stories flow out, effortlessly one hopes. Each person is a stranger now but by 10:30 a.m. I will have been given a peek into their souls...

At this very moment I can see trees out the window and a piece of blue sky, which shows we live on mother earth together, and see the same sun, the same stars...

Ten Things I Love To Do

1. Eat Chinese food 2. Dance wildly 3. Go barefoot
4. Write Haiku 5. Walk by the seashore

6. Plant & harvest vegetables & flowers 7. Pet my cat 8. Read an old journal 9. Drink really good coffee 10. Braid my long hair

A Turning Point On My Time-Line

When my grandmother died on the eve of my 14th year, it had a huge effect on me. My beloved Baba, who gave me my first diary when I turned 12, Baba who loved me unconditionally, lay in a casket, her smile stilled forever. I wanted to say Baba, wake up, don't leave me! Someone had pinned a pink camellia on her peasant blouse. I wanted to say, be alive Baba, like this flower. My first published poem, when I was 18 and in college, was about Baba's death, which still haunted me.

I believe Baba, who taught me to love life and follow my principles, to be true to myself, will never really die, for she lives on in me and in her great grandchild, Alana, and in the 12 camellia trees I've planted in my garden.

Leaf And Self Portrait Haiku

Polka dotted leaf
who painted your green body
just to make me smile

One hydrangea leaf
delicate ridged edges clipped
by a green scissors

Sitting with flowers
pen in hand, among women
fulfilling a dream

This moment is all
my pen needs to speak
wisdom
from my heart outward

Once Upon A Time - A Seed Story

Given phrases are in italics.

Once upon a time a little mermaid sat on a rock in the vast ocean, dreaming of becoming a writer. No one in her large mermaid family seemed to crave being an author, they were content to dive in and out of the waves or comb their lustrous long hair as they lay out in the warm sun. Today was the day, Merrilee decided. She plucked the precious pen out of the top of her tail – she'd found it floating days before – and picked up a board that had cradled itself near her rock. Ah, this was the moment.

"*I close my eyes,*" she told herself, to put herself in a trance. Then she asked, "*What's in the silence?*" She heard not only the waves lapping and the gulls crying, but the music in her own head.

Merrilee put the pen tip down on the board, opened her eyes, and waited. She knew that *stories flow out* if you trust in your powers. Sure enough a poem inscribed itself on the grain of the wood. She knew it was only the beginning of her long career.

In fact, in later years, Merrilee would start her own press and invite other mermaids to join in, till a vast library of mermaid literature was born.

One Of Life's Great Pleasures

One of life's great pleasures is my cat Georgie, who I rescued and adopted when he slunk into my yard a few years ago looking piteous, full of worms and fleas and scars from life on the streets. Georgie, who meets my car whenever I arrive home, who follows me around the yard when I'm planting or harvesting flowers, or weeding, or pruning, or just sitting in the Adirondack chair with a cup of iced coffee, reading a magazine or writing haiku in my journal. He stretches out in front of me on the grass, then turns over to expose his white tummy.

Georgie is what is called a ginger cat. He's orange with rust colored stripes, four white paws and a white vest. He is a very handsome fellow, and a rascal, who while I'm petting him decides he's had enough and swipes me with his big paw. Other times, when I'm on my screened- in porch in my wicker rocking chair, reading, he jumps in my lap, kneads my legs with his claws, then settles in for a comfy nap, purring with a big throaty rattle. In my short stories, I try to include Georgie as often as I can – I mean, what's a good story without a cat? -- but in those stories, I call him Odin, who is father of the Norse gods. What can I say? I adore him!

Name Acrostic

K aleidoscopic mind

A lways creating word patterns

T aking the time to plant flowers, saying

Y es to love, and

A sking to hear your stories

Haiku

Hands, with me since birth

doing everything I ask

never saying no

My life is a book

I can't stop reading – each page

new to these old eyes

Cast of Characters

I am a dancer. I believe I danced in the womb, and once I was free of limitation, I danced on this earth. Moving my body was not a need for exercise, but for self-expression. I danced eyes closed; I danced around bonfires; I danced at my wedding; I danced with my newborn daughter.

I dance in my dreams. I dance naked, I dance with veils, I dance in company, I dance alone. I will dance even on my deathbed as I go through the curtain to the other side, to a lush green meadow filled with wildflowers that I will tuck into my long white braids, and there I will dance until my next incarnation.

Freedom Acrostic

F eel your inner strength

R eap the harvest of your hard work

E njoy the sun, rain, moon and stars

E nter your own version of heaven

D on't believe falsehoods

O beautiful woman, look into love's

M irror

At This Very Moment

At this very moment we gather for our last formal class. I look around at the women who I've shared this classroom with for six weeks. It feels so much longer, as if we have known each other in a cosmic sense, a timeless sense, our pens connecting us, our laughter and tears, our insights, poetic utterances, our willingness to open to each other's wisdom. At this very moment I feel the gift of our hours together, as one feels the gift of a glorious sunny day or an exquisite bouquet of flowers. We are that day, we are the rainbow flowers blooming.

Why I Write

I write to relieve my mind. To get images out of my head. To help myself get my imagination working. To brainstorm thoughts. To vent my bad feelings to the paper instead of being judged on what I say out loud. I've learned in my writing class how to be even more creative. Ms. Taylor challenges me and I like that!

Alishia

I have so many thoughts and feelings going on inside of me! I just need to slow them down a bit so I can make sense of it all, which is why I write. Often times writing slows me down OK, but not always. There are those times when my mind flows faster than my pen. At that point it's almost pointless to write 'cause you can't read the chicken scratch anyway! But I digress. When writing about what's going on in my amazing mind, it gives me the opportunity to take my feelings out literally and be able to look at them. I'm also able to articulate things that I could never say face to face. It's a safe journey to sharing me!

Mahlona

I've always enjoyed writing, good with words, putting pen to paper has always come easily to me. I write so that I can free my mind and tell my secrets. When I have something difficult, embarrassing, or emotional that my brain and body cannot process, my hand can wield a pen and clarify it all. I write so that I can learn who I am. I write so that I can live freely, despite fences, despite iron bars, despite locked doors. Writing sets me free.

Sophie

I write to see my thoughts. Sometimes I talk to myself to hear my thoughts but writing retains the spirit on paper. When I get in a particularly dark mood I write to vent. Because when I'm in those dark moods I can look back and see the confusion on paper. It's a good process for me because when I find those old moments on paper I can laugh at myself. It helps me to remember how perfectly imperfect I am.

Victoria

I write to live. I write to breathe, to be, to explore my spirit. I write to flow blood into the veins of my alter ego, expressing my epiphanies, desires and disasters. I write because to not do so, I could not exist.

Susanna

I love the freedom and the words as they describe my life. They are written pictures of things good and bad, and all that lives in my head. I can see patterns and cycles and things that I don't notice. When I write I feel like a famous poet. My deepest fears and loves and everything in between, all in black and white waiting to be seen. Freedom from capture are the thoughts I feel. Always when I write my words are full of zeal. Words touch others like nothing else can. They comfort my child and soothe my man. Thank God for words, and for expression from within.

Peppa

I write to express myself. That is why I write when I am sad or happy or hopeful. Someday I might write a book to tell my story. There are things that have happened to me that others need to hear so they can learn from them. Most of all I believe writing leaves a legacy of one's life that should be shared with the world. That is why I write.

Charlene

I write because this is how I am best able to express myself. I am unable to keep my train of thought if I'm speaking. But if I can write it down instead of stammering or stuttering or doubting myself, suddenly I am eloquent, articulate, even insightful. Writing allows me to reveal a part of myself that you would otherwise probably not see.

Melinda

I write for many reasons. I would say the best thing about writing is that I am able to go back to special memorable times that will live in my heart forever. Some say once time passes you can never turn back the clock, but I disagree. Our minds help us to escape where we are, allowing us to relieve happy times in the past. I write to hold on to hope, I write to remind myself of God's promises and to remind others who may be at a low place in life that we are strong, and not to give up. It is easy to become despondent but there is always hope. No matter where you may be, by writing, you can go any place you wish...

Billi-Jo

I write to eliminate confusion, I write to delve into the mystery of things, I write for the joy of it. I write to share my thoughts, feelings and visions with others. I write to explore what it is to be human, to live out my arc upon the earth. I write to leave a trace of myself to live on when I am gone.

Katya

196

IMAGINATIONS
UNCOVERED

Writings of women at FCI

Fall 2015

FCI: Fall 2015

This anthology is the last of the women's writings from FCI, as of Fall 2015. When Prison Wisdom *is published, a real book I can hold in my hand, I have every intention of returning to FCI and writing again with a new class. For now, I pay homage to the women whose creative works are excerpted below. Each student's writings, prose and poetry, are collected together. Cover graphic drawn with pencil by Mysti.*

MYSTI

I Am A Woman Who

I am a woman who has lost everything, even my own words, yet rises again and again. Just call me Phoenix as I burn it all down only to be reborn. I am a woman who has been broken, twisted and bent into an intricate knotted sculpture. One that resembles a beautifully scarred heart. I am a woman who has been abused yet can still be gentle, who knows how to love and be loved. I am a woman who has failed then danced on the shards of her own broken dreams. I am a woman lost then found. I am a woman seeking redemption. A martyr who at times is the savior. I'm homemade apple pie with wild cherry flavor.

If My Life Were A Book

If my life were a book it would cross genres. Just imagine if A Requiem for a Dream met A Clockwork Orange then fell in love with The Princess Bride, had a baby and named it after its uncles Pulp Fiction and Rock-n-Rolla. Then you might begin to have some idea of my past experiences. If my life were a book it would be that one way back on the shelf that hardly anyone has read but has become a cult classic to those who have. The margins would be covered in illustrations like tattoos on time on skin. There would be darkness and light and passages of forgotten memories. It would be visceral and uniquely tactile in feel. The censors might call it dangerous but you dear reader know it's only real. Most of all, it would be open, the pages dog-eared and well worn with love. The shocks long since absorbed and incorporated as life lessons both light and dark, best held and finally let go.

If I Were A Piece Of Furniture

If I were a piece of furniture, I would be baroque in style, have many ornate carvings and myriad dark colors. I would have layers of light and dark woods. I would be a deep dark chest holding many secrets, with hidden drawers and panels only I know the mysteries of. I would bear the scent of ancients in my woods and oils.

Haiku

Thoughts of you and me
luminosities red sky
how we say goodbye

Imagination, An Acrostic

I mmortality

M agnified

A westruck

I dentified

N ow integrated

A nd owned

T aken to higher levels of

I nnovation

O ne's innocence is outstretched

N ow newly inspired to create

Freedom Acrostic

F aithfully waited

R esolved to discover again

E verything

E ver

D reamed of doing while locked away,
   for this

O ne

M oment in time

Character From Another Time Period

I am the wise woman of my clan. I live in the highlands of Scotland. As a people we are oppressed by the English yet always we fight for our freedom and our gods. I live in a small hut that is built into the side of the mountain. At the back of my wee little home is a hidden door that leads to the caverns. We use the caverns to hide our men from the English dogs. I also use one of the chambers as a storage room for my herbs, tinctures and my precious scrolls and tablets. I've got long red hair, green eyes, and alabaster skin. I'm not married as most of the men folk fear my powers, but I'm not evil, I'm just wise in the weirding ways. I was born with a caul over my face and me gran said she saw the faery lights all around the house when me Ma was birthing me. Me da says I'm a natural with a bow and a knife. I'm a bit fierce with a stave as well. I learned to read the runes from me gran when I was a wee lass. There was never a hurt animal or man me ma couldn't patch right up and all her healing secrets she passed to me. When I can't grow or hunt up for meself I trade me tinctures and a throw a the stones for. Of course all the village girls come to find out who they'll wed someday. I'm alone atop of me mountain, but I've no time to be lonely. Besides I've got old Fergus, my wee black cat for company…

Name Acrostic

M elancholy moments

Y earning for release

S eeking divinity

T earing down the walls

I nnocence becoming integrity

At This Very Moment

At this very moment I am filled with hope for the future. And terrified to fall again. I am aware of every heart beating in this room – each adding its own distinct *pa rum pa pum pum* to the melody of the universe. I am painfully aware of my own uniqueness and the fact that in and of itself it is nothing less than mundane, as we are all uniquely one. At this very moment I know that somewhere a star has burst into being while in another galaxy an old one dies. I am in awe of the intricacies of the cosmos and infatuated with the simplicity of life... of love. I am grateful for second chances and new opportunities in life... in love.

KEISHA

I Take Myself To A Beautiful Place

It's a special place. It's warm and cozy. It can get cold and icy, but for the most part it's gentle and kind. It's breathtaking and refreshing all at the same time. It's captivating and rejuvenating, it leaves you speechless. Its love is unconditional and when I am there, there's no place I would rather be. I feel very special to have the key to this place. It's wonderful knowing that I can go there at any time of day or night. This beautiful place is my husband's strong, loving arms.

My Hands

My hands are gifted. They shampoo hair, they color hair, they curl hair, they style hair. At times they become very dry from all the chemicals and water they encounter, but that's when I walk them into the nail salon and let my nails feel care for them. At home I use special lotions to help with the dryness. I really have to take time for these hands because to me that's what one notices first. Besides I have a husband who took these hands and vowed to love me, therefore I must keep them together, for me and others too.

I Love To Cook

I love cooking because I love to hear other people tell me how much they enjoyed their meal. I like going to the grocery store, picking out all the ingredients needed for my meal, coming home, lighting some candles, turning on some music, and preparing the food. I like looking at recipes and making small changes that I feel make the food taste better. I enjoy taking my time when cooking, not being in a rush. I enjoy going out, getting nice plateware, glassware, silverware, depending on the occasion and decorating the table, then spreading the food out, and watching everyone eat, come back for seconds and thirds. Then when it's all over they tell me how wonderful it tasted!

If I Were

If I were an animal, I would be a fish. I would love to swim around all day and explore the deep blue ocean, getting a chance to see all that lays below, that world unknown.

If I were a piece of furniture I would be that beautiful uniquely made mirror that hangs on the wall with a wonderful brown leather trimming. I would catch the eye of everyone, not just to admire my beauty but also to admire theirs.

Far Into The Future

In the crowd I stand up on a platform. Ladies are clapping, smiling, some crying as they listen to me. They love feeling rejuvenated, empowered, and free. My words will be the topic of conversations. One will always love to see me enter a room, loving to have a candid conversation with me. Telling others about me, encouraging them to come out and listen to me for themselves. The knowledge I will express will be powerful, leaving others to want to know and hear more. Every time there is an empowering convention in town that's where you will want to be, somewhere in the room listening to me. This is what I foresee in the future, me empowering the lovely ladies to be all they can be.

Cabin In The Woods - A Guided Visualization

One fall afternoon, I was in need of a little me time, so I decided to take a little walk. I was walking down the long country road, then veered off on to a pathway, which led to a field of lovely flowers. I was amazed by their beauty and the sweet bird songs that were in the air. I continued to walk further into the valley of flowers when all of a sudden I saw a little cottage sitting there. I sashayed over to the door, and turned the knob. It opened, and I then entered the cabin, looking around. It seemed abandoned, no signs of anyone living there. As I turned to walk back out, I saw a black trunk sitting there, and it caught my eye. Instantly I became curious. I walked over to the dusty trunk and lifted the top. Inside was one's Wedding Day Memories. There was a photo album of their happy day. Also laying inside was the cake top, tux, and a wedding gown. As I lifted the wedding dress, there lying underneath was a black velvet box. I laid the dress aside to open the box. Inside were the most dazzling, beautiful pair of diamond earrings. They looked to be about four or five carats. I made my way out the door, walking back through the valley. I keep opening the box to admire the beautiful earrings, thinking how they once looked on the bride on her day of happiness.

Haiku

Self Portrait

Sometimes it is fire
sometimes it is like a breeze
I am always me

At This Moment Now

At this moment now
learning new ways to write
never will forget

I Am A Woman Who

I am a woman who loves God, I am a woman who has many gifts, strength, wisdom, and knowledge to share. Walking in my shoes has caused me to change quite a few times, depending on the walk. I was walking from high heels to pumps, to sneakers, to slippers, each pair of shoes having its own race to run.

Through all my walking, I must say that being humble has carried me a long way. Being open minded to change, and willing to accept the things that I could not change. Taking responsibility for my own actions, being honest even when it hurts. Over the years I've learned to have gratitude, and always give respect because I want it in return.

Letter From My Older Self

Dear Keisha, I sit down today to write you a few words about life. Life is a gift that should never be taken for granted. Always show gratitude and be humble. Be thankful for everything and be anxious for nothing. You always want to be a woman of integrity, doing what's right. There are other young women out there who will look at you and will need some guidance. Speak words of wisdom to them, helping them to understand and be grateful. Know that you are special, always know your worth. Remember that you can do anything you set your mind to, giving it 100%, never half. Always keep God first, with Him all things are possible. There's a time and a place for everything, and you are in that place.

A Shimmering Image

This moment was beautiful. I had waited so long for this day to arrive. Planning for this day brought tears and laughter. I never knew that it took so much to prepare for this life- changing adventure. Phone conversations that not always went well, all day shopping with appointments lined up back-to-back, food tasting affairs, colors to check and approve. Many different personalities coming together, and all coming into agreement on a variety of things. I felt like superwoman. And in the end, it was all worth it, walking down that aisle, looking into his sexy brown eyes, holding his hand, saying yes to becoming Mrs. Williams.

DONICIA

My Hands

My hands are my very own. They are not like any one else's. People see me as different which I'm learning to accept. It's OK to ask why are my hands different from yours? This is the way my God made me! Most everything I do is unique in its own very special way. Everything from tying my shoes, to sweeping and mopping the floor is different from you. Yet God gives me strength to guide me through all the rough spots in life. I'm not the same as you. Nope!! It's okay that God made all of our hands different. Black, white, yellow hands, most with ten fingers. But mine only have five. Today I say to the world, here I am, take me as my Heavenly Father made me! If I can do things different, and there is someone out there just like me that is afraid, I'm here to help them know that it is OK! To show them life goes on. Just reach for God, and he will help you to overcome it all.

Leaf Haiku

This fall soon shall end
next year I'll be home laughing
kicking up the leaves

Self Portrait Haiku

Smiling cause I can
loving others as I am
knowing this won't end

Mother Haiku

Growing up so fast
many separated days
no more tears to cry

Timing must be right
our pathways must be aligned
joy growing within

I Remember A Room

I remember a room so very clearly, like it was yesterday. I lived in this room for so many years, if these walls could talk they'd tell you some stories. In this room was my life. Pictures of the ones I held so dear to my heart. Some days were awesome, laughing and joking, yet at the end of the night that was very different. A lonely time, very quiet and dark, no one's here, it's only me and my thoughts. Why have I chosen this life? The money, abuse and drugs, are not worth this pain. As I push past my weary thoughts to fall asleep, on a magic moment I dream of the day I can be with my family and children, as my pictures of them come alive in my head, their warm touch and a bear hug from my son. This laughing is the love laughter that is like no other. True love that comes from deep in my heart. Family always did love me and missed me all these years. So why did I walk away? COUNT TIME! I am awakened by the voice of the C.O. yelling. And I smile because I know that this dream is soon to be my reality come true. Soon I will walk in the door of the place I call home now and be surrounded by all the people I love the most...

When I Look In The Mirror I See

When I look in the mirror I see blond hair, blue eyes that are like my grandpa's. I see a smile like my mom and a nose like my dad. I'm one of a kind and I know my face has changed over the years. Once so young yet I know I'm learning with age as I grow older. I'm mature now and still have a lot to learn. I am beautiful and smart. I have a caring and sincere heart. I smile even when I don't care to and laugh even when it hurts. I always try to see the brighter things in life, which God has given unto me. I'm a child of God, a daughter of two great parents! I have a big family with many siblings. I'm a sister, a mother of two amazing kids. I'm a believer that at this end is my beginning to eternal life that awaits me in heaven. I'm a leader of my own kind, I've got a voice that matters. I can't wait for this new start. As I get prepared from God, I hear his voice saying you're almost there, keep pushing, strive for the best, and show the world what I'm about. Without God I wouldn't even be looking in this mirror today...

So, Here I Am

Sitting in this class, behind these walls and barbed wire fences. Yet I know that I am free! Free on the inside to be me. Some people think Oh My God, I'm in prison and therefore lost. But I've found myself here and with all that has gone on, I'm still alive.

I know God has a bright future waiting for me. I'm so very excited yet I wait calmly and patiently for my day to come so that I may shine oh so bright like the star that I know I am. There are many stars in the sky, but I'm the only one like me. God knows my name and he knows the numbers of hairs on my head. Without God where would I be? God has quieted me through it all, so that I shall succeed in His name!

I Am A Woman Who

I am a woman who has been through a lot. Yet not for a lost cause.

I've been down and as yet I still manage to get back up and try again! I've been through the fire, tested and tried, though I still grow inside.

I'm learning to fly.

I have an amazing family, two beautiful children, and many stories to tell. As I wait to go home I work on myself. As we are told, I must first clean out my dirty cups from the inside out, and as this is my goal, my cup is starting to look clean. So I'll be able to set it with other sparkling clean dishes, yet mine has a crack and some chips in it, to remind me of the trials.

I will not forget my power because it's what makes me who I am today.

I am a woman who fears the most high God as I await my time to shine. My purpose of this life has many meanings, but above all else, the will of the Father is my main reason for living.

TANYA

Self Portrait Haiku

Daughter, sister, mom
no laws can take that away
this is who I am

Leaf Haiku

Beautiful fall day
crunchy brown leaves on the ground
hear the children laugh

At This Moment Now Haiku

At this moment now
all walls are being torn down
possibilities

Character From Another Time Period

If I could be a character from another time period, I would be an Egyptian archeologist of old. Wearing the customary white linen, with a big straw hat. Even suffering through malaria and other diseases, just so I could say I've been digging along the Nile…

I would love to experience digging in the earth and extracting a surprise in every handful of sand. I would try to solve the mysteries that took place so long ago by decoding ancient text, and cataloging artifacts. The best though would be sleeping under the same stars as Cleopatra, King Tut, Isis, and all other Egyptians from thousands of years past…

If I Were A Piece Of Furniture

If I were a piece of furniture I would be a table. Like a table I have many functions. I am a mother, sibling, daughter, friend, companion, and I am stable. I can be depended upon to do all of these roles independently but most time simultaneously. I am also strong, balanced, and sturdy, and that allows me to be the person I am for myself and others who need me.

My Hands

My hands are like no others. They are uniquely mine. Within my hands are many powers. The power to build or the power to destroy. The power to soothe or the power to cause pain. The power to capture or the power to release. Of all the powers that my hands hold, the power to pray is the greatest of them all.

It Was The Night Of The Full Moon - A Fantasy

It was the night of the full moon and Jakuri slowly made her way between the huts as everyone else prepared for the celebration. What am I doing? she asked herself for the 100th time. If I get caught, Chief Lion will have me married off before the sun rises.

Tonight my tribe was to celebrate the passage of the boys into manhood. There were no girls or women allowed until after the ceremony was complete, and of course all they got to do was dance and do the work of feeding the men. But I was not going to help. I was going to prove that I could be a warrior too!

I had already cut off my braided hair and caked my face and head with the red mud that the warriors wore. All I needed now was to find a spear and shield and I would be ready to join the hunt. I would kill the biggest animal and feed the entire village...

I Remember A Room

I remember a room that changed my life. When I walked into the room, I walked in as a girl who believed the world was full of kindness, love, and that anything was possible. I was 17 years old, in a hospital room, about to give birth to my first child. I was happy but afraid, uncertain, unprepared. It was a lonely time. I had been sheltered all of my life and now I was entering into a whole different world. Motherhood was quickly approaching. The birth of my daughter was a magic moment. Not only because this perfect little being came from me, but because at the moment of her birth, the way I viewed the world changed. I was now someone who loved more than myself, a woman who was willing to fight to protect her child from all that was waiting for her in the world...

A Letter To Myself, 20 Years Older

Dear Tanya, It feels like only moments ago that you were just 44! The last twenty years have certainly been a journey. There have been many mountains to climb and far too few valleys of rest. But you are stronger now for all of your travels. There is no doubt whatever that you are prepared for what likes ahead. Don't waste time trying to live in the past. Those days are gone, but so many lie ahead of you. Remember that saying you love: *"Cherish yesterday, dream tomorrow, live today."*

Haiku

At Golden Arches
slinging burgers, my first job
quit after one week

I Love To Read

I love to read because it allows me a few moments to get outside of myself. I get to meet new people, travel to foreign lands, and do things like climb mountains, herd sheep, explore islands, and other adventures that I've never had a chance to actually do. I love to read because sometimes someone else's story can make me look at my own story differently and with gratitude instead of negativity. Reading allows me to have some time with myself in a place where being alone is difficult. When I read, I can forget temporarily about any problems, stress, difficulties that I have, and just be free to enjoy that time wherever I have been taken to....

Freedom Acrostic

F ought for

R elease

E arned

E nlightenment

D ignity

O vercoming obstacles

M ercy

PATRICIA

I Am A Woman Who

I am a woman who sky dives, scuba dives, and surfs. I'm drawn to the ocean, the smells of the sea, the sounds of waves crashing against the shore rocks, or the subtle calmness of the current. I am a woman who appreciates the explosive force of the ocean and the levels of beauty it contains.

I see that the ocean is the source of life for many. It is the source of undiscovered medicinal treatment; it is the source of employment. It preserves the history of the world.

I am a woman who appreciates the sight and beauty of an erupting volcano on the ocean floor in Hawaii and watch in awe as the ocean expands and creates a new island, and how lava cools, where the ocean collides with it.

Shimmering Image As A Child

I remember when, as a child, I was playing at a park in Los Angeles. The place was familiar to me because it was an after-school program and I walked to this park and took lessons in tennis and gymnastics.

One day I was sitting on a bench and having a snack, when a man walked up and sat down beside me. I looked at him, and although I had never met him before, I instantly knew him. He had warm eyes and appeared to be very kind. It was at that time he introduced himself as my natural father. He went into great detail as to why I was living with the family who were responsible for me.

As it turned out, he and my adoptive parents were great friends, and my adoption had a lot to do with the scrutiny that my natural parents were under in the Soviet Union. So I was transported out very young as the daughter of an Irish couple, to have a better life out of the Soviet system.

We became very close after the fall of communism, and saw each other frequently. He died in Los Angeles in 2004.

Leaf Haiku

Large brown spotted leaf
fallen from your lofty perch
windblown to and fro

Fall leaf all alone
on the cool wet morning grass
sits in idle sleep

Once Upon A Time ~ A Seed Story

A stormy Sunday afternoon, tears and laughter, she taught me

Once upon a time, in the middle of the journey of life, I came upon a muse. She appeared to be gliding along as she walked. Her feet looked to be moving effortlessly like she was walking on clouds. There was mist all around. I will never forget this meeting with the muse, as it was following a stormy Sunday afternoon.

I watched her for a time and thought to myself that she must be with others that I couldn't see, because you could hear tears and laughter echoing through the woods. She came upon me and initially I was intimidated, because she was beautiful and was surrounded by an aura of happiness.

When I worked up the courage to say hello, I also asked why she was laughing at times and crying. I asked if she was with others. She said that she had tripped over a rock and stubbed her toe. So she had tears and laughter over her clumsiness. She taught me that sometimes you just have to laugh at yourself, even to the point of crying.

Self Portrait Haiku ~ Two Versions

Ships sail as sun sets
by the island where I sit
through troubled waters

Life sails against seas
crashing on a troubled shore
sunset breaks, then peace

A Favorite Meal

The times of life that I cherish are the times when the family comes together to cook a favorite meal. It is not the taste of the food, or the spices used, it is the preparation and the atmosphere in the kitchen as each person works on their respective dish.

Mom might be peeling potatoes, telling a story on how she didn't have a potato peeler in the old days. My sister might be making a soup, laughing at mom, because we've heard that story a hundred times, and each time we hear it, the story becomes a little more embellished.

At the end of the day, the meal is ready, and we gather around the table to hear dad tell his story about how his first gift to mom in 1938 was a potato peeler. This of course would be the same utensil she claims never to have owned in the "old" days.

Character From Another Time Period

In another life I am an art restorer. I studied the old masters in Florence, Italy and have an apprenticeship in Venice. I have the ability to look at any piece of art and from the brush strokes tell you if it's a Vermeer or a Da Vinci. I'm commissioned to clean and restore these masterworks by the churches of Italy or wealthy patrons. It can take me years to complete a commissioned piece, but I'm treated well by my patron and live well. Restoring old masterpieces is peaceful and allows you to appreciate the skills of long ago.

I travel to my commissioned work and I travel light. I have my art supplies and clothing and nothing more. Restoration is a serious and tedious work. Much depends on the quality of the canvas, and where the painting has been hanging. Various chemicals are needed to clear an old portrait and much linen. Each piece of linen is to be placed into the chemical only once, then dabbed on the canvas only once to remove the gum and build up.

The removal may take me months because there is no electricity. I can only work by natural light, and I move the portrait as the sun moves, illuminating shadows that can obscure the work.

My patron checks on my progress weekly but I intentionally drag out the commission to last longer than necessary, because it's my bread and butter, free lodging, and three meals a day. It's a charmed life.

I Take Myself To A Beautiful Place

It's a place like no other. You can wade out into the water so warm and blue, and when you look down at your feet you can see tropical fish passing. You can walk miles down the shore and never encounter another person. It's quiet except for the sound of the ocean. As you pass a set of banyan trees on the shoreline, your breath is taken away by what lays just beyond – a large swath of black sand beach. The sand is soft despite the fact that the black sand is from ancient lava.

I sit on the beach all day. I listen to the waves pound against the cliffs and shelf just beyond. The sun drops lower into the sea and I begin to walk again. I don't have far to go. By now the sun is gone and I'm at a very small point, but it's a dramatic spot on the beach at this time. The view is of lava dropping into the sea from Kilauea Volcano, on the Big Island of Hawaii.

CAROL

My Hands

My hands tell the story of my life. They are getting older now and are beginning to show it. My hands are scarred from the life I've lived and each scar tells a wonderfully unique story. My hands are very strong and provide me with the ability to be independent and to support my family. They are calloused from years of hard work but loving and soft at the same time. My left hand wears a wedding band that was placed there 28 years ago by my loving husband, and my right hand allows my creativity to flow through this pen today.

Both my hands are attached to my arms, and I love to fill them with my loved ones. In moments of misguided anger my hands may hold up a one finger salute, but thankfully I have learned to control this feeling with age. My hands welcome strangers with a firm shake.

I Remember A Room

I remember a room, not because it is a special room, nor for its beauty. In fact it is a boring and ugly room, with its white metal 8 x 8 partition walls. I have spent over a year in this room and it has been a very long and lonely time, with no one to hug or to kiss, and my family a thousand miles away. For this reason I have grown to hate this room, but I will never forget it. This room is never dark and rarely ever quiet, as there are many, many others here just like it, full of women, like me, who would much rather be somewhere else. But because of our own poor decisions we are all prisoners of this room. Until that magic moment when they say we are free, we will continue to live our daily lives in this room. True, I have grown to hate this room, but I will never forget it. It is because of this room that I have learned extremely valuable lessons. Like to never take my freedoms for granted. To appreciate all those little things in life that we all seem too busy to even notice. To live my life every day to the fullest for myself and my family. To make all my future decisions with this room in mind. I will always remember this room for what it has taught me.

My Favorite Meal

I prepare my favorite meal only once a year. It takes a full day and a half to complete – but it really isn't about eating at all. After all the gifts have been opened, and everyone has visited their in-laws, step-families, extended families, and friends, they all head to my house, knowing that should come hungry and with nothing in hand. Everyone we know is invited and this gathering is our gift to them. Family, children, neighbors, old friends and new, the more the merrier. I share with all the recipes passed down from my family's generations past, present, and future, prepared with all my love. Each year the menu is the same with the occasional new addition. My great grandmother's spiral ham recipe, glazed with a honey, brown sugar, cherry and pineapple juice concoction, covered with sliced pineapples held in place with whole cloves and a maraschino cherry in the middle. And a huge glazed peppercorn medley turkey breast, complimented with my grandmother's cornbread stuffing with fresh celery, caramelized onions, and garnished with a walnut cranberry sauce. My mother's sweet yams with golden brown marshmallows on top. My sisters loaded mashed potato casserole with tons of bacon, cheese, sour cream and chives. My very own broccoli and cheese casserole with a tiny kick of jalapeños, and my triple layer banana pudding with my special ingredients – crushed pineapple in the pudding and topped with French vanilla Cool Whip. As I have passed along these recipes to my daughter, she has since incorporated her homemade from scratch pecan pie recipe, that she now brings with her each year for our annual family Christmas dinner. Before we begin, we all gather in the kitchen, holding hands through to the living room and the formal dining room, back into and around the kitchen, as my father-in-law blesses the meal and all who have gathered.

Do not get me wrong – I am no Betty Crocker or Martha Stewart, but I can follow a recipe. This family tradition is ten years old and will reconvene in December of 2017. I welcome you all to join me and our family in Texas. Bon appetit!

A Milestone Moment

It was a time when we were so young and in love, facing the world as a united soul. We worked two jobs each of us for over a year to pay for all the precious little details. Our future unknown, we didn't care as long as we were together. Our daughter like a barefoot princess leaving a trail of rose petals, my white gown following me through the garden aisles, while he waited at the end, clad in his tuxedo. Flowers all abloom and their sweet fragrance thick in the air. Too hot in Texas, in July, but blessed with a beautiful non-rainy day. Friends and family joined to witness and celebrate our union. Many milestone moments have come since then. We will soon celebrate our 30th! I am so blessed after all the years to want to say "I do" all over again.

Leaf Haiku

Brown magnolia leaf
once green and fragrant, alive
now fallen and found

Curly leaf, dry, brown
details like a fingerprint
no others like it

Self Portrait Acrostic

C aring by nature

A ngel wings my symbol of faith

R ealist by virtue

O ptimistic by character

L oyal beyond fault

When I Look In The Mirror I See

When I look in the mirror I see a hint of the young woman I used to be. At times I see my mother from a few years past. And I know in the future, I will see the memories of my grandmother staring back at me. When I look in the mirror I see, on the outside, freckles, acne scarred, and sun damaged skin with hazel eyes that change color from the brightest green to golden honey. I see long hair that is honey colored also with a few persistent grays that return pluck after pluck. Full lips that are slowly learning to smile more frequently than frown. A nose that is slightly too big, a reminder of my American Indian heritage. Wrinkles on my forehead, around my eyes and mouth, a constant reminder of the hurdles of my life. Permanent make-up on my eyelids and lips – what was I thinking? A scar on my neck from one of many surgeries to correct my spinal deterioration. Strong shoulders that at times seem to hold the world.

When I look in the mirror I see (on the inside), a wonderful mother, much better than the one I had. An absolutely devoted wife, a loving sister and an always loyal and honest friend. A fiercely strong woman who amazes me daily. A woman whose inner beauty is only matched by her kindness. A powerful survivor of all life has thrown my way. An optimist through to my soul, who is always capable of finding the silver lined cloud even in the worst of storms. I see a woman who is as serious as she is goofy, who finds strength in her own weaknesses, and who loves to help others up after they have fallen down.

ANGELA

So, Here I Am

So, here I am, surrounded by beautiful women learning different ways to be creative in expressing one's thoughts. Although we are in a prison setting, our creative writing class at this very moment allows our minds to be free and escape the barb wire and day to day routine that comes along with being in bondage. So far we have shared different ideas, laughter and tears. I look forward to the weeks ahead. I believe we will get to know each other more intimately and learn so many wonderful techniques of writing from our dear teacher. She has taken time out of her life to share her gift with us, shedding a little light in our dark world.

I Am A Woman Who

I am a woman who loves God, my parents, siblings, only darling son, and friends. I try to see the good in everyone. I am a woman who is so loyal to the ones she holds dear to her heart. In fact sometimes too loyal to those who aren't even worthy of her loyalty. I am a woman who has been through many hard trials and tribulations but I have always found a way to persevere in spite of. I am a woman who doesn't harbor ill feelings or allow the terrible trait of jealousy to attach to me. I am a woman who loves to travel and see the world, gain insight about different countries and cultures. I am a woman who loves to swim. I think I'm a mermaid at times because my body is so in sync with the water. I am a woman who never allows the facts to outweigh my faith. When one door closes a window will open. If the window closes the roof will fly off. There's always a way – it just takes patience, something I'm developing day by day…. I am a woman who is eternally grateful for life and wake up every morning with expectancy in my heart.

A Shimmering Image

When I was a child I played Althea Gibson in a play for Black History month. You couldn't tell me anything. I had on a white tennis skirt and white polo shirt pressed to a crisp. My sun visor was white as well, with my long hair hanging over it. Usually my mother kept my hair in ponytails or braids, but this day it was blown and pressed out. Tied around my shoulders was a red, blue and white cardigan. And in my right hand I held my tennis racket. I gave my speech and did a twirl with so much enthusiasm until I won the entire auditorium over. Everyone cheered, laughed and clapped. That just gave me more fuel. I even swung my racket a couple times. Althea Gibson may have won the Wimbledon, but I won the entire school over that day. I will never forget how parents and teachers kept coming up telling me how great a job I'd done, and they couldn't believe I wasn't nervous. I really felt like a super tennis star!

Leaf Haiku

Spotty in color
long lines like a fingerprint
not a hand but leaf

The season has changed
limbs do the walk with the wind
leaves are everywhere

Brown, sturdy and firm
this leaf stood the test of time
may I do so too

Self Portrait Haiku

Determined and strong
smart, driven and witty too
the make up of me

At This Moment Now

At this moment now
I have laughed and shared haiku
never to forget

Mother Haiku

Precious gift given
go to the end of the earth
never ending love

My bundle of joy
some tears other times laughter
never would I trade

Acrostic Poetry

Self Portrait

A ims for the sky

N ever gives up

G od fearing

E xpectant mindset

L oves everyone

A lways there when
    you need her

Freedom

F inally

R evealed

E nchanting

E xhilarating

D itching

O ppressed

M ode

Cabin In The Woods - A Guided Visualization

Walking through the meadow on an unusually beautiful afternoon, the breeze felt especially calm to my skin. I looked and saw a strong eagle soaring across the sky. My eyes followed him until he was out of distance. Oh how I envied that eagle flying high above the clouds. The meadow ended and the forest began. I could hear birds chirping and the leaves crunching beneath my feet. As I continued on my path I could see an old cabin ahead. I wondered what could be in the cabin. It looked as if it hadn't been occupied in years. With every step the stairs creaked. I peeked in the window. There was so much dust I was sure my allergies would flare up, but if I didn't take the chance of entering I would never know if what I was looking for was there. I opened the door and some chips of wood hit the floor. I swatted my way through thick cobwebs. And there it was, over in a corner, the secret chest I've heard about so many times over Thanksgiving dinner but no one believed it existed. I lifted the latches, my heart beginning to race. I took a deep breath and opened the heavy lid. Holding it with one hand, I retrieved the mysterious photo album. I leaped for joy and ran out the cabin, running through the leaves, anxiously trying to reach the meadow. So many thoughts raced through my mind. Is this the real thing? How awesome it would be to present my great grandmother's album and family tree at this year's Thanksgiving dinner.

I Take Myself To A Beautiful Place

Old San Juan is rich in historic views. From the coffee and cigar shops to the ruggedness of the roads. However, my favorite place in Old San Juan is the rocky piers overlooking the ocean. This is the most breathtaking view I've witnessed thus far. The sound of the waves crashing against the rocks, children in the distance playing basketball on the other side of the pier, the ocean in all its array of blue spreading on into infinity. Different yachts and boats skating gracefully across its body. The clear sky overlooking it as a mother who watches her child. The sun reflecting its rays and smiling on the water. I could go on and on about this peaceful view, but it's one I suggest you witness for yourself.

KATYA

At This Very Moment

At this very moment a new class begins, in a flurry, as finally all students are settled in. The flowers glow brightly on my desk, and the pens move without stopping on the first blank page of our journals. Looking around the room I see a group of women, each one a stranger (except for myself of course), and yet by the end of these two hours I will already feel connected, the warmth of our sharing lightening the cold fall day. At this very moment I praise what is yet to come, the unknown adventure stories, the tears and laughter, as we take off every mask and reveal our true face.

I Love To

I love to write poetry. I joke that I was born with a pen in my hand but it feels true. From earliest memory I was scribbling little stories and poems. As I grew older I found that writing poetry was a special way I could access my feelings, and in just a few rhythmic phrases communicate that emotion with others. My first published poem, in a college literary magazine, when I was 19, was about my beloved grandmother Baba dying of cancer. While it had happened five years earlier, my sadness lingered, and writing a poem seemed to not just express the sadness, but in an alchemical way, to transform it. I have written hundreds, maybe thousands of poems, but the one I am writing now, whatever its topic, is magical, because it is newborn, and nothing like it has ever existed before…

If I Were An Animal

If I were an animal I would be a tabby cat with a plume of a tail, and the softest fur. My mistress would adore me, feed me delicious morsels, give me a soft pillow to sleep on, and a garden to play in. In return I would let her pet me, and I would reward her with a contented purr. In fact I would be adept at cat language and have a large meow vocabulary.

Once Upon A Time: A Seed Story

A *stormy Sunday afternoon, tears and laughter, she taught me*

Once upon a time, on a stormy Sunday afternoon, a little kangaroo sat behind a hillock whose height protected everything but her tail, although she tried wrapping it tightly around her shivering body. All of her kangaroo family had gone off to the annual jamboree, but little Kuku was not in a social mood and did not care to be around all the tears and laughter, the pounding of all the kangaroo clans big strong feet, and the general hullabaloo. Little Kuku was sensitive, you see, and secretly she was writing her first book of poetry. For that she needed solitude. As the rain crashed all around her, she picked up her fountain pen (bequeathed to her by her grandmother) ready to begin a new poem. Kuku thought to herself "She taught me," (referring to her grandmother) "to always listen for the inner silence," in order for poems to be born. Kuku's heart lifted, the rain slowed to a drizzle, and the poem flowed out unhindered into her notebook. At that moment, a ray of sun broke through the clouds, Kuku unwrapped her tail, and stepped out into a glowing world.

Shimmering Image As A Teenager

I loved to sing, and in junior high I auditioned and was accepted to a girls chorus called The Harmonettes. We all wore blue (blouses, skirts or a dress) and black shoes. The image I am thinking of now is when we went to sing, close to Christmas, for the patients in a nursing home. I was only 15, with my whole life before me. As we, The Harmonettes, stood all in a line in the nursing home's common room, I looked out at a sea of old people, most in wheel chairs, some half asleep, others with eager smiles on their faces, I felt tears come to my eyes. I sang with more sweetness and passion than ever before, longing to bring joy to these aged souls. I'll never forget singing the soprano part for *Silent Night, Holy Night*, and tears slowly slipping down my smooth, young face.

Leaf Haiku

Bright gold autumn leaf
your life is almost over
yet you shine for me

Self Portrait Haiku

Writer from the start
stories flow within like blood
my pen knows them all

At This Moment Now Haiku

At this moment now
we've become Haiku poets
magic we can share

Acrostic Poetry

Self Portrait

K imono wearing woman

A lways a pen in her hand

T ranslating feelings into words

Y ou know she wants to understand

A ll of life's mysteries

Imagination

I pick up my pen

M eaning to tell my story

A live with all possibility

G aining wisdom as

I write

N ever blocking the truth

A sking to be of benefit

I llustrating one human's

O riginal

N ovel of life

Freedom

F lying over any obstacle

R eveling in the unknown

E ntering a dream state

E xerting one's inmost powers

D o not give up

O pening yourself to this

M agnificence

I Take Myself To A Beautiful Place

I'm in an old-growth redwood forest near Mendocino, California. It's the last day of a dance camp retreat and my husband Tom and I decide to take a 45 minute hike to an icon at the top of a mountain, called simply *The Big Tree.* The path is steep and we stop every so often to rest. Finally we make it to a small clearing, where a hand painted wooden sign lets us know we have arrived. We've already been told that this giant redwood is over one thousand years old. Long ago, lightning had carved a portal, a sculptured gate, in the front of the enormous tree, smoothed by rain and wind, chiseled ornately, as if to say *"All who enter here will be enlightened."*

Tom puts his head into the hollow, and says, "Katya, you could stand up in here!"

I enter the tree. I hold my breath, overcome by emotion. The redwood's energy fills me with a vibration unlike anything I've ever experienced. For a few magical moments I too have lived the life cycle of that giant being, I too am one thousand years old, and still growing.

"HEXAGRAM" ART

Each student was given the same materials to create an image on a yellow construction paper rectangle: three blue "sticks," two green triangles, a red circle, a smaller white circle, and one paste-on star. Once they had decided on a layout, they glued the pieces down. Only then were they asked to give their design a title.

I have found over the many years of offering this exercise to students that no two "hexagrams" (my term for this evocative form) are ever the same. Although there are only eight pieces to arrange on a background, each artist expresses her own unique voice, just as she does in her writing.

I share five examples with you here.

One Goal – Different Paths   Tanya

Star Shield   Mysti

A Chance in Time   Angela

Light in the Forest   Katya

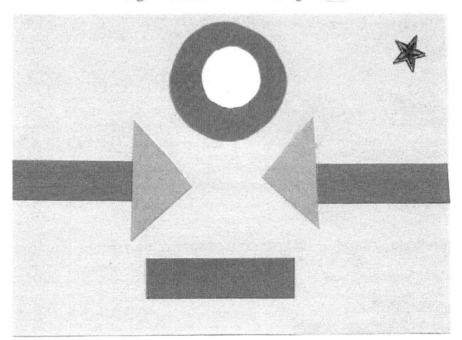

Always a Way Out   Kiesha

Seed Phrases and Exercises

The purpose of this glossary is to assist anyone who wishes to offer writing classes, whether to prison inmates or to any other population. These time-tested phrases and exercises are intended to evoke material (stories, poems) hidden inside, waiting to be expressed. If students are assured that they "can't do anything wrong" and that they are the only ones who can write their own story, success is assured. It is of deep value for teachers to write with the students—encouraging open sharing and self-acceptance—rather than set oneself apart.

SEED PROMPTS

At this very moment

So, here I am

When I look in the mirror I see

I remember a room

Sometimes I feel, or Sometimes I wish

Sometimes I forget

If my life were a book

A day by the sea

Once I traveled

A rainy day

Ten years ago

A childhood friend

A fantasy vacation

If I lived to be 100

If I had the time

My favorite time of day

Once I dreamed

A current obsession

A favorite pair of shoes

If I were an animal

Starting over

A precious object

Once I lost, or Once I found

My hands

A lonely time

A magic moment

When I was a child

One of life's great pleasures

I am a woman who (I am a man who)

I was born

A favorite meal

A favorite garment

Saying goodbye

EXERCISES

Ten things I love to do (expand on one)

Today in the 3rd person (today she knew, today the man woke up...etc.)

List of 5 accomplishments (choose one to expand on)

Write about a mythological person in your life

Turning points or milestone events (childhood, teenager, adult)

Listening to music and "free writing"

The following exercises fall under the category of fantasy or fable, encouraging the imagination:

It was the night of the full moon...

I enter the scene (looking at a photo/illustration from a calendar/magazine, etc.)

I take myself to a beautiful place

I find myself in a room I've never been before

The Essence Exercise (If I were an animal, a piece of furniture, a garment, etc.)

The Two Noun Story (i.e. partners choose, share, make title of (i.e. Rain Slipper)

Animal and inanimate object fable (partners choose, share—i.e. the elephant and the saxophone—and fable begins "*Once upon a time...*")

Guided Visualization (The cabin in the woods, Message in a bottle, Talking to a wise being, e.g. in a rocking chair on a cabin porch)

POETRY

Haiku

A three-line Japanese "essence" poem of 3 lines, with a 5-7-5 syllable
count, often focusing on nature, the seasons, and the range
of human emotion
Leaf, flower or other natural object haiku
Spring (or summer, fall, winter) haiku
Self-portrait haiku
At this moment now haiku

Acrostic   Using a word, i.e. WINTER, or FREEDOM and creating
a poem using each letter as the beginning of a new line

i.e.   T ick tock

I t never stops

M y life zooms by

E ven as I write this poem

I AM   Poem using a ready-made structure (I am, I feel, I worry, etc.)

Age poem   "In my 38th (fill in your own) year of life..." Based on Lucille
Clifton's poem

"I have seen"   Based on Walt Whitman's poetry

"So much depends" Based on William Carlos Williams' poetry

Five Noun Poem – five words are picked that must be
included in the poem:
i.e. rain, moon, sorrow, joy, flower

Suggested Template For The First Class Of A Writing Workshop

If in a prison setting, have journals ready for each student with lined pages and a blank cover. Place nature scenes from calendars or magazines on top, and ask students to choose their seat based on which picture appeals to them. Use glue sticks to paste down pictures. If not in prison, students will bring their own journals.

Use file cards folded over for names (use sharpie markers) to put on desk for each student. In my classes, students are allowed/encouraged to use their first names. Check with prison to see if appropriate. Make sure to have pencils available as well.

Intro:
Assure participants that "this is not a writing contest, no one can write your story but you." Explain there will be no critiquing. Everyone shares, everyone listens with full attention. Share that "seed phrases" and other exercise prompts will be given to help get the pen (or pencil) moving.

First prompt: *At this very moment...* (I usually do not have people share this writing, until later, if they choose to.)

Second: *Ten things I love to do...* (make list, then choose one to expand on). Everyone shares, including the teacher/facilitator.

Third: *I remember a room...* Share.

Fourth: *Name Acrostic* (see anthologies for examples). Share. If more time in the class period, two more suggestions for seed phrases: *Solitude* or *A favorite meal.*

Closing Circle: At end of first class, have each student share (going in a circle so people won't have to decide when to speak) *one thing of value they are taking away from today's session.* I usually share last, and validate the group experience.

SECTION II: PEN PALS

Pastel drawing by Frank Walls, death row

Introduction

Why have I chosen to correspond with prisoners? It all began more than 50 years ago when I wrote letters back and forth to Robert Kingston, whose story has already been shared here, including the reason I have dedicated this book to him. Our friendship, our *kinship*, deeply impacted me.

I have always appreciated the intimacy of correspondence, a qualitatively different medium than phone calls, emails, or texts. Letters allow a deep sharing of ideas and feelings. There is time for reflection before responding. The fact that prisoners write with pen or pencil, not with typewriters or computers, enhances the sense of connection. Holding a letter in one's hand, reading it at one's leisure, creates an atmosphere of rapt attention.

Of course, my pen pals are all people who have entered my heart. Writing to them is not a matter of being altruistic or "feeling sorry" for them. It is about nurturing and being nurtured. I have purposely not included much of my own writing in this section; I wanted instead to focus on their gifts to me. I want to reveal, by sharing their words and art, their unique personalities and character, and why I have chosen to stay connected to them, through letters, all these years.

Receiving a real letter in my mailbox is a boon. Receiving the art my correspondents have created is a rare and treasured gift. How poignant that these individuals have chosen to confide in me, to share their talent, their hopes and confusions, and how poignant that I am able to do the same. I am all too aware that these men and women are or have been incarcerated behind bars, and that I walk free in this world. And yet... and yet...we share something that goes beyond these constraints; we inhabit a reality without limits when we put pen to paper. We take off our masks. We see not just the facts of our identities (black, brown, white, male, female, old, young) but our spirits, who we are and who we are becoming.

I give thanks to the pen pals in *Prison Wisdom* for enriching my life. And now it is my pleasure to introduce them to you.

Gallery of Pen Pals

Robert Kingston

(Donald) David Dillbeck

Frank Walls

Misty McCray Romero

Leonard Scovens

Martin Rivers

Marcia Suttenberg

Katya Sabaroff Taylor

Robert Kingston

The story of how I met Kingston appears in the Prologue of this book. As I have already noted, it is unlikely I would ever have offered writing to inmates if it were not for this gentle, artistic, and philosophical individual who gifted me with his unconditional friendship. I was only 18 (and he was 29) when I met him on the streets of New York City, and I was able to reunite with him when he was released on parole "for good behavior," after he had served half of his twelve-year sentence. Though we were separated geographically, we continued to write until he died of emphysema shortly after my daughter was born. The two letters of mine that I am including in this collection were written when I was 19 and 24 years of age. Most of Kingston's correspondence to me has been lost, but the one letter (and several works of art) that I still have in my possession are shared with you now.

Hello Rainbow,

I've been thinking of green fields – I think if I am ever to do any worshipping I will do it in the fields or hills or on the shore or sea where one can see and feel the beauty of nature's manifestations. I can feel very reverent in the field even though it is an imaginary one. I could never feel this reverence in the traditional church. You can understand this I know. My mother is very sweet and thinks that church services of the ministers would comfort me. If I were a less complex man perhaps this would be so. Being as I am I don't seek comfort. I seek knowledge. Knowledge of man and man's acts – knowledge of the fact and principles of reality and of human nature and conduct – and the principles underlying the arts, the sciences and the like (psychology, sociology, philosophy, etc.)

I am learning and I am growing in mentality and I feel this is the important factor in my life. Also I feel that I have cultivated a taste for aesthetics, if not for religion. All this is because of you. You have gotten through to me somehow, no one else ever has. By being so alive, you have given me life. Please remember this when you feel unhappy or apathetic. You are the beautiful woman who lives in the mist of my dreams. She is and you are much too beautiful to ever be unhappy.

Your letter came last night. I did the wild flowers then. Wanted to do something for you. At first I did others in a vase, but I didn't care for them in a vessel, too much like sacrifices. Then I thought I'd do one flower for you of delicate beauty and charm, something very tasteful. I didn't feel that this was right either, for it wasn't me. So I'm sending you these very common wild flowers. Or rather my "perception" of them. I think perception is the word I want for I am trying to give a sense impression of the flowers, accompanied by an understanding of what they are. And they are a very common weed bursting violently into the sun, the flowers shouting Freedom! Joy! Love! Knowledge.

And the reason is you.

I have some oils and small canvas panels coming. And soon I will lovingly bombard you with paintings. Wish I knew how to tell you how much I love you.

Bob

P.S. Have you heard Peter, Paul and Mary's The Answer is Blowing in the Wind?

Wildflowers painted on lined notebook paper

Dear Kingston -

It is always such a pleasure to see your handiwork, especially the drawing of hands, both the ones I've got on the wall and the new set I received today. Your red nude was remarkable. The face seemed quite characteristic of your man Modigliani. The body was beautifully done. It is with avid attention that I read your remarks concerning your own drawing. I see a fierceness of purpose that you lacked before you began drawing again in earnest. You are not just protesting now; you are shouting with careful precision and illustrating your most important concepts. Please always continue to send me what you do.

I feel so far from everything and I am much in need of you, silly that I should need you now perhaps as much as you've once needed me. I am happy oh really happy that your art is taking such a firm place in your life. Your art can be your goddess now, for I feel as if I at present fail for that position. I want so badly to create, to write poetry, to reach the eyes and souls of men, of Kingstons and lovely sad people, to build myself in words, on paper, in meter....

Now it is my turn, isn't it, to ask forgiveness for melancholy demonstrations. But this is life, a turn to the left and a twist to the right, sometimes failing, sometimes achieving, sometimes loving, sometimes aching. ...

I want to be with you, to let your arms help my ache by encircling me, to let your branches lean over the stream and gently brush the mossy banks, the carved polished stones. Oh dear I do love you so, and I shall write poetry once more. Give me some time and I shall come to. I really will, I promise you. And meanwhile, please care for my rainbow, keep it in its satin gold-edged box, wrap it gently at night, and tuck it under your pillow ...

1963, age 19
at Antioch College

Day of Freedom

Dearest Bob,

With ink smudged hands, I love you too. To receive your letter on Nov 12 saying *I am going home on Nov 12.* My first incredible thought is not even *Now I can see Kingston,* but the even more astonishing sensation of *Now I can talk to Kingston on the telephone!*

One needs so slowly to accustom one's senses to these added dimensions. I could dial your number right now... or you could right now as I compose words, be dialing me. I am very tempted but my shyness wins out, and I'm afraid the loudness (the actual sound) of our voices would shock us.... You must be shocked to walk unnoticed down the city streets! and eating dinner with your mother! The biggest freedoms... are they the smallest? I wish you'd keep a journal now. And painting.

I'm overwhelmed *with* you... I hardly know how best to rejoice. Somehow with tenderness, with honest frightened (because so new) joy for you. You You You

Can we go slowly which means letting all this freedom seep into our pores? It is so delicious! Kingston, are you really there, are you there are you there? My God here it is, the long awaited.

Write me quickly, slowly, like a free man, like who you are... and then, soon, let's talk to each other, OK?

Written on Liberation News Service stationery, 1968 I was 24 and working as a journalist

Kingston at the beach during my visit after his release from prison

Dearest Kayta Nina,

I read your poems and I am completely covered with a warmth that lasts without time and without distance.

When I was in prison, your words, the images that changed me and touched me where I lived, filling all the dry spaces inside me with amber light and bright sirens of color —

I love you.

Kingston

Self-Portrait and letter from Kingston after being paroled

Vive la bagatellé !

A happy birthday card to me from Kingston
in colored pencils

248

(Donald) David Dillbeck

I had recently moved to Tallahassee and was reading the local paper, when I saw a front-page story about a prison inmate, out on a work detail, who had attempted to escape and killed a woman at a shopping mall parking lot.

Such crimes often end up on the front page, and while these stories always make me very sad, I found myself staring at the black and white photo of the man who was being charged with murder. Something about his image reminded me of my old friend Kingston. Was it his eyes, which seemed to look right into mine?

I heard about an organization, Kindred Spirits Charitable Trust, which helped find pen-pals for inmates on death row. I spoke to a woman who was able to give me Dillbeck's mailing address. I wrote to him, he answered, and, as of this date, David and I have been corresponding for more than twenty years.

Perhaps from reading excerpts from his letters, and the fable that appears at the end of this book, you can believe that a human being can be redeemed and may also help others by sharing his own hard-earned wisdom.

Flowers painted by David on envelopes of letters he sent me.

January, 1992

Dear Donald,

I spent many years in Oregon and the ocean, the Pacific Ocean, always inspires me in its rugged beauty. This photo is actually of California where I spent my childhood but Oregon is still my favorite memory of the sea.

Of course you don't know me. My name is Katya. I followed your story in the newspaper and always felt, since I first saw your photo, that you were a sensitive person with a lot of feeling for life. Now that you are in prison again you must feel cut-off and alone. Perhaps through some contact with the outside world, in letters, you could recapture a sense of hope and connectedness.

Donald, when I was only 18, I met a man on the streets of New York City who later went to prison. We corresponded for many years. His friendship enriched my life as we shared our life stories with one another.

Are you interested in having a correspondent?

How do you keep body and soul together day by day? Do you read, keep a journal?

I am teaching a class in journaling at the Leon County Jail. The men and women have written powerful and poetic pieces about their memories and seem to gain a sense of purpose through writing. If you are interested, I can tell you more about this.

Sincerely,
Katya Taylor

Katya, the interview lasted about ten minutes. I had written out a statement because I don't have a lot of experience giving speeches, and what I wanted to say, I would have forgotten half of it with perhaps nervousness. So I read my speech and somewhat shocked them because one lady said they weren't used to anyone being that extensive. I knew that most people say they are innocent or want to blame everyone but themselves and all of this pretty well goes on deaf ears. They have heard it all 1,000 times. A couple days later they came or rather had an officer come to get the page I read from and wanted a copy of it. I am going to share with you now what I told them.

"I first came to prison at the age of 15. I was a victim due to being told I was going to stay locked up, anywhere from 25 years to life. For a teenager, that was forever. I couldn't see beyond my own situation. I felt like I was the one being done completely wrong, I thought my sentence was unfair. All I could think of was getting out and being free.

Eleven years later I escaped. I was in a very paranoid and panicked state of mind and in the course I took another human being's life from them. I can't offer you any excuses because I was completely wrong and I'm fully responsible. No one else is.

I'm not only responsible for two people losing their lives, but also a tremendous amount of pain and suffering their families have felt. A wife had to go on with her life without her husband. Two boys grew up without their father. Then a husband lost his wife and the grandchildren were not able to know their grandmother or her being at home alive. Seems like way more punishment to me than dying. Once I die my own punishment will be over with. My suffering is over with. But my mother who must live through this will be the one truly hurt. She is the one who will experience the loss. She is the one who is truly being punished.

For myself, I can't ask for mercy because I don't believe I deserve it, but I do believe it's completely unfair to my mother who has never done anything wrong but love me.

252

Please take this into consideration. Thank you."

So Katya, that is what I told them. I wanted it to be something that they were completely not expecting and different from what they normally get, and I hope this delivered. As well they realized this came from the heart. I'm sure many other things could have been said as well, but I thought this is what would make the biggest impression. I know not to expect any positive results but for my mother's sake, I had to at least try.

When I was in open population, and was around 23, I took a business education class, mostly to learn how to type rather than do the slow two finger process. In this class I did learn a lot, not all from the teacher's words, but it was a place I learned to think. In the classroom she had a very nice book on photography, a subject that has always held a fascination for me, from the first camera I was given or seeing old black and white photos that seemed so magical to me seeing back in history. Anyway, in this book there were some real neat pictures where the shutter was opened for a longer period of time. I believe the process is called stop-frame. And it can make a butterfly travel across a page and you see the blurry process, or see stars streak across the sky over night and it looks like one second. Such pictures wowed me, due to such a trick of time, it helped me to think of time differently than the day to day. And at least with the mind's lens rather than just one brief second of time, why not see the whole process? Now only the now of this second but why not look at your whole life in one flash or even yet why can't you include all your ancestors and children as one line. Time is very much an illusion. Why can't this illusion be changed by our perception?

Back in the early 80's I was taking a college course and they were held in the evenings. I was sitting out on a sidewalk just gazing out at some trees on the other side of the prison fence. The sun was setting and I saw how beautiful everything was, and the thought came to me, I wish I could own such land. And a deeper part of my being surfaced and said all that I see I already own. I believe there is a truth here. We don't possess it, but we are a part of the earth. There really isn't any separation. What we see, what we love, is also a part of us.

About life on death row.

I get out of this cell two times a week for up to three hours at a time for yard. And take a shower three times a week anywhere from ten to fifteen minutes. Other than that, I'm in this cell 24-7.

David's birthday card message to me.

Hello to the soon to be birthday girl. Tell me this, do you ever think about all your ancestors, as well as Alana and future offspring that are to come? On your birthday you being a connector of this long thread of women? All the roles they played. Their happiness as well as sadness, pleasure and sorrow that touched each one and made them who they are and also is part of your make up to a degree as you will be to the future clan of women. Whether we feel it or are aware of such a line, we are a part of it as it is a part of us. I'm embracing all of you as one right now Katya.

Katya, in this beautiful card, you wrote about how you haven't been as regular with writing me as you would like, because you are out in your garden or reading library books or writing 700 word stories, cooking, etc. etc. Well, whether I get a letter from you regularly I feel very safe in the knowledge that I do live inside your heart, that such a place is home. I'm fully aware you have a life out there. I love it that you love being in your garden. I know the value of being connected to the earth, putting your hands in the soil, having desire for your plants to grow big and strong, allowing a part of yourself to be mixed with the flowers. Oh this is truly wondrous! Next time you are out there, please put your hands deep into the soil, close your eyes, and think of me doing this with your hands, and Katya, you doing this will be worth 100 letters to me.

Lately, I've become way more aware of air. And have become good friend with air. Air is always so overlooked or seen right through as if air doesn't exist. Air has a great sense of humor, has quite an adventurous curiosity and goes everywhere, loves us to give attention, and once we really become aware of air there is a playfulness there as well. There isn't any space , crack or cranny that air doesn't enjoy exploring, breathing in and out, air goes here and there, everywhere.

Katya, I feel truly blessed that you saw my photo in the paper and were inspired to write me via Kindred Spirits. Sometimes we make a choice not thinking much of it, and it turns out to be something wonderful. I'm closing my eyes and reaching out to you as that woman while you are looking at that photo. And I'm embracing you. And I'm whispering in your ear, thank you!

Everyone in prison knows longing, yearning and always wanting what is kept away from us – all that we are denied. We desire freedom, intimacy, action or numerous other ways longing and desire is manifested. Longing for what we don't have is a constant companion. We all know it well.

On this compound there are a handful of old oak trees that must have been around for a very long time. This prison is over 100 years old and I believe the oaks have been here way longer than that.

There is one that is kind of out of the way on the prison grounds that inmates have access to, but I think many never give it much attention.

After being here for a little while for some reason I felt drawn to the spot. So I would often go sit under it and watch the goings-on of the hustle and bustle of prison life. Watching others interact with each other while constantly letting the words "Watch, listen, learn and observe" repeating themselves over and over in my mind. This really gave me a calming affect. Whenever I had free time I would do this.

One summer day when it was hot and I was tired of dealing with the heat, I went and sat down at my favorite spot enjoying the coolness of the shade and hearing the birds sing above me. I decided to lean back against the oak and before I knew it I was asleep.

I found myself dreaming that I was no longer a man, but rather I was the oak. I felt my roots go deep down into the ground, spreading out, receiving nourishment from the soil as well as water from the depths. My trunk felt solid and firm, and my branches reached high up to the sky, and my leaves freely fluttered in the breeze, taking in sunlight. All of this at one time. A tree content to just be where it was. No anxiety, no rush, no urgency to be elsewhere, fully alive. And as I woke up I heard my inner voice say "This is BEING, this is wholeness."

The oak and I share a kinship. And even though I'm human I feel like this sturdy friend has taught me a lot about my self. I may not have roots but still I'm grounded in the awareness that I'm as much the earth as any tree. I don't have a trunk yet I'm capable of being centered and solid in character, and as the leaves are focused on the sun, I too can be focused on the light that gives us our life. I've become calmer. Yes, I still have longings and would like to experience things I'm not able to. I know it's okay to be where I am – having pleasure in simply being my self.

So if you are in prison, trapped in unfavorable circumstances, don't be afraid to sit under a tree because you just never know how this may change you. Who knows, you may even find this freedom inside you, not outside, and sometimes dreams do come true.

> I was surprised to read that David could sit under a tree, while on death row, so I asked him to explain the letter in which he talks about his meditation under an old oak tree in the prison yard.
> This is his reply:

No, I can't sit under any trees here on the row. I'm on concrete 24-7. The rec yard is pure concrete, is shaped like a slice of pie probably 40 feet wide and 90 feet long.

That little story had two combinations as inspiration. I spent most of 1979 to 1986 at a prison called Sumter (in central Florida). On that compound there were walkways , and one of them had a tree next to it. Sunday mornings when most of the other prisoners would be sleeping in, I would often get up to go to the canteen and buy a pint carton of orange juice and a fruit pie, which I had the canteen worker heat up for me in the microwave. And I would then go sit under this tree and just watch all the goings on and yes the words "Watch, Listen, Learn and Observe" were constantly my thoughts. I did pick up quite a bit of human behavior on these Sunday morning retreats under this tree. I don't remember if it was an oak or not. I just remember the Spanish moss, reminding me of my favorite weeping willow trees.

The second part of this story is I do have a meditation where I am an oak tree. Just letting my awareness be filled with contemplation of being an oak, roots, tree, branches, leaves, the whole of One. What gave me this idea to start doing this I'm not sure, but it is something that is very calming …

Look Into The Eyes of Wisdom

Look into the eyes of wisdom
Look into the eyes of love
Whatever you are looking for
you can find behind these two doors.
They are open and inviting, even enticing
A mystic dance into the iris
A flame to the highest.
These eyes tell it all.
the words that cannot be spoken
The truth that cannot be broken
Every nationality is able to see
life's hidden mysteries.
So come, come, come
Passion beckons,
the chains are broken
Delusions no longer smoking
We swim inside the ocean
deeper and deeper
Brighter is the light
The fight has been won
Life has just begun.

*I had included an I AM poem in one of my letters to David. He wrote back
with one of his own.*

I am the diver who seeks the soundless
I am the motion of a twirling dance
I am the laughter of the child
I am the dog who chases his tail round and round
I am the wind both in the calm and the hurricane
I am most of all I am
I am the morning
I am the night
I am the earth, the sky, low and high
I am the infant's first breath
I am the sigh of the elder's last breath.
I am all, I am One.

Dear little butterfly

The one who flutters her wings by the pen and paper…

After reading a few times about your encounter with the little bird friend, I thought about how nice it was for it to allow you to take care of him/her. Here is a poem that is close to that bird's life and death.

Look at the bird with golden wings
See the eyes that can tell the untold
As he stretches his wings with a mighty cry
He rises up to the sky, not even caring how high
For he is not afraid to die
He is the bird with golden wings
Such beauty and splendor radiates from him
His body is a temple for a great spirit within
He knows the secret path to the hidden gate.
Watch him, watch him
He's the bird with golden wings.
No company does he cry for,
Nor will you ever hear him blame fate
His life is a dance, so festive is he
His song is just to sing the sound of Creation.

My letter responding to David's poem.

After reading your beautiful letter on my sunny front porch today…the yellow winged bird poem and accompanying words of wisdom…I was struck by the irony – is that the right word? – of our special correspondence. How the "world" would see my writing a Death Row inmate as an act of kindness, to bring some light into your prison cell, whereas in fact you beam rays of such gentle and pure energy my way with such regularity and grace that I am often resurrected from the "prison cell" of my own doubts and confusions, as you part the curtain or blow dust off my vision's window. Thank you David. I guess we can acknowledge the equality of our gift to one another, and at least I hope I can shine both my light and my concerns, fears and questions, my divine and mortal self inextricably braided – in your consciousness as you return with your own storehouse of selves….

Dear Katya,

Hello my gentle, affectionate, kind, wise and tender soul.

I just had a visitor. I am not sure if he visited me and came to my world or I visited him and came to his world.

He is a friend to all of us and has been since our journey of mankind started. He is none other than the candle flame. There have been countless times throughout centuries that we have come to him for understanding, insight and comfort. All the campfires and candles have given us so much wisdom and inspiration, a reflection of our own soul. Fire is so beautiful and a lifeline to all of us. Without him we could not live, but also he brings us to the door of death and destruction, only where new birth can arise from the very ashes.

Are we all not phenomena, playing inside the endless flame. In it we find pleasure and pain, tears and laughter, yin and yang, good and bad, love and hate, creation and destruction, yes and no. All of our very forms of polarities, all as being One...

Another flower, David's envelope art

260

OK, you ask can I dress up in my mind in some fantastic costume? Now that you ask I will. I shall dress up as the wind, moving here and there, being the movement of trees lifting higher, and embracing the clouds, then re-entering close to land, moving in and out of every human being, every animal and plant. Letting birds soar inside me while I experience their experience, then I experience everything that every being is expressing: good, bad, indifferent, and finally the earth herself.

After all of this, I will tire of pretending to be the wind and I will look and see a man who is writing someone very dear to him a letter. I will then pretend to be him. He lives in two prisons, maybe even more that he is not aware of. One of cement, barb wire and iron bars. And another of flesh and blood that is caught up in time and space. Now I find pretending to be him very humorous, because I forget that I am only pretending, and as I forget so does he. If you will, laugh at the poor fool for believing that he is confined, when all the while he is free, only playing the role of prisoner!!

Along in yesterday's mail came a very big surprise, one that I never would have even guessed being cleared by the mailroom. I was sent three rose petals in a letter. I have not touched a flower in so long, just touching a petal is a very wonderful experience. Holding it up to my nose and sharing its delightful fragrance is also great! I now only wish I could experience the flower in its wholeness. Not to be picked or possessed but to be admired and to share my own flower-like quality of being with it.

The rose shares her petals with me allowing me to touch her essence even in death, knowing that she lives in the gesture of a friend giving to another. The simpleness of love and change. What a blessing!

I knew there was something to Spirituality and I wondered how could I learn to make this energy to bring results when I wanted it to. To be able to harness instead of it being something of randomness, and for this I wanted to find a teacher.

After being arrested I thought well finding a teacher is shot all to hell. But life always makes its own demands on our heart's desires, bringing them about in ways that we would least expect. I had no inkling about the transformation that was about to take place and I would find it in a jail cell.

I was an avid reader and picked up a book called "Huey" about a Vietnam helicopter pilot, that was full of questions. His life had been turned upside down and he wanted answers that chaplains could not answer nor any of his friends. He then met a man who brought him to a Buddhist monk and the monk showed him with simplicity that the answers are inside him, not out. Reading this began to open the doors of my destiny.

I then had the idea why not call up a church or organization that might be affiliated with Zen. I found a person that used to attend Unity Church that became a simple teacher, one that would show me unconditional love and teach me how to untie all the knots of my past, to let the ghosts and shadows of the mind be put to rest. And introduced me to the life of mysticism. And now you know the rest.

Would I have pursued a spiritual quest if I had not lived such an unbalanced life in the early stages of my life? I do not know. Would I have if I had not screwed up my life in so many ways as well as others. I do not know. What is to know is that my life has unfolded as it has, and I stand as I stand because of it. It is a story of sadness and triumph, even in the presence of such despair.

So here we are, two people, two souls, celebrating the beginning of awakenings. The beginning of transformation, of finding the presence and source within. We celebrate our heavens, we celebrate our hells, the opening of harmony and the colors of chaos. life is easy, life is hard, but it's always our life to make of it however we will.

How many times have we been here before? How many times shall we be here again?? Does it matter? No. What a wonderful play it is, to be a part of all this manifestation.

David with his mother

Frank Walls

Kindred Spirits Charitable Trust, an organization that matches pen pals with death row inmates, sent me Frank Walls' name when I requested a new pen pal.

Frank is another example of a self-taught prison artist. The colored pencil and pastel drawings he has shared with me are remarkable, as you shall see. It is his flower painting that appears on the cover of *Prison Wisdom*.

Being on death row can break anyone's spirit, and Frank has struggled through the constant reminder that he could be signed next for execution. Yet despite this, he has managed to create art of beauty and sensitivity.

I have chosen to showcase his art, but have also included one of his letters that portrays his caring and sensitivity.

As of this writing, death warrants are currently on hold, as the State of Florida wrestles with technicalities. I hope that Frank has found a measure of peace and will keep on creating with his magic pencils and brushes.

This is one of Frank's letters from 2007, giving insight into his character.

Dear Katya,

It's always a source of comfort and a wonderful blessing to receive your letters. I received your birthday card with the heron on front, and your letter. I apologize for my slow response. My body is having a rough time adjusting to my workout program. I'm working out five days a week (Mon-Fri) and take the weekends off. I've changed my sleeping pattern as well. I go to bed between 11 and 11:30, instead of staying up really late (2–3 am) or staying up all night. I'm getting up early in the morning and readjusting my daily schedule to incorporate my work out program. It was rough at first, but I'm adjusting. I'm really enjoying the cooler temperatures, better sleeping weather!

How have you been doing? I hope to find you and your loved ones doing well and in good health. Give Tom and Alana my best regards. Big hugs for you all.

Now, in response to your birthday card. You mentioned that you put in for a subscription to a magazine called *Birds and Blooms*. I received a notification card from the company, confirming that you requested and paid for a subscription on my behalf. I'll let you know when the first issue arrives. In the meantime, thank you! It really sounds like I'm going to enjoy this magazine as a source of inspiration to my artistic and spiritual talent. Again, thank you so much!

The visit with my parents, as always, was great! Other than being in the embrace of God's eternal Love and Salvation there is no other comforting feeling than to have mom and dad's arms around me and hearing the words, "I love you my son."

Bertha has been in my thoughts and prayers! I am a believer in prayer. I wish that I could go visit her, read some scriptures with her, pray with her, and just spend time with her playing Scrabble. Anything to make her feel loved and to lift up her spirits....

Ninety-three years old! I pray that I reach that age. It's good that she is getting lots of visits. I sure can understand how comforting visits can be – although I only get one or two visits per year.

I loved the colorful poetry piece about ancient rain... I like the added touch with the cut out leaves, really accentuating the meaning and vision behind the poem. You write beautifully, Katya. You have a very beautiful mind!

I'll close with big hugs.

Sincerely, Frank

Colorful flowers
blanketing an open field
a heavenly sight

Such tranquil beauty
shared by birds and butterflies
God's gifts to the earth

A warm and sunny day
light upon nature's garden
nurtured by God's love

May we be thankful
and count all of the blessings
bestowed upon us

This is one of my favorite paintings of Frank's. I can smell the fragrant flowers and hear the birds singing.

Birds in a flowering meadow

Frank's Mama horse and Baby in a field of flowers

Smiling Giraffe

Frank's fawn in the forest

*This is the rest of the fawn picture,
Mom leaping the fence*

Frank has asked me to include his mailing address so that if readers wish, they can contact him. Here it is:

Frank A. Walls # 112850, Union Correctional Institution, P 6109
PO Box 1000
Raiford, Florida, 32083

Misty McCray Romero

Photo by her husband Matt Romero

When I first began teaching women at the federal prison in Tallahassee, one of my students, Misty McCray, was a young woman who revealed not only a sincere devotion to writing, but to her own re-creation. She decided, when the course was over, to keep a writing group going for other inmates who had taken the LifeStories class (at FCI, inmates are given the opportunity to offer classes to each other). I gave her a copy of my book *Journal Adventure Guidebook* to use as an aide in her teaching.

Two years went by. One day I received an email from Misty. She had been released after eight years in prison and was living in Jacksonville. Could she write to me? I was very happy to learn that she was no longer incarcerated and was now making a life for herself. She hoped to be a motivational speaker and to use her writing talent to uplift others. We kept in touch and sometimes wrote stories together (from a common seed prompt). Life on the outside proved challenging, and she had her ups and downs.

Finally, she met a fine young man and fell in love. She asked me and my husband Tom to come to her wedding as witnesses.

Since that happy day, Misty and I have stayed in close touch. She is a remarkable young woman who has grown exponentially since we met six years ago. As she shares eloquently in the following pages, she used her time in prison to overcome a negative world view and to refashion her life, a life where she can now give back to others.

Here is an excerpt from Misty's very first class with me, to the seed phrase: "So, here I am".

"Creativity, I can hear it beginning to awaken out of its sleep. Rise women and share. Let the beauty of your strengths and weakness emerge. Write!"

2010

Misty and I began writing two-noun stories from the same prompts. Following are two examples. These pieces, and the ones that follow, will give you insight into her process of overcoming obstacles and re-emerging as a confident and focused woman, dedicated to sharing her story with others.

Mirror Record

"Mirror record" is what one finds in their mind and what they see looking back at them. A record of what has been, what is, and what will be. Listen to the record. Dare to peer into the melody of your soul. What will you find, and is it worthy of playing or should you change the tune?

These are the thoughts Myra held in her head as she stood staring at herself, now a woman with experience. She had troubling years and had overcome them. A woman with integrity and ambitions was once a lost little girl.

The mirror shows signs of aging and tousled hair. A blemish here and there. But these are no longer the things Myra focuses on. She sees so much deeper than the exterior. She no longer points out all the flaws and mistakes. She doesn't notice the pain that used to grip her, with clenching fists, holding her captive. Maybe these images are what drove her to fight. Fight for her life. Myra, like so many, had a low image of herself and was dying inside. She wanted so badly to believe she was worth more. So she dared to look at herself. She decided, starring at a blurry reflection of herself in a jail cell mirror eight years ago, to face these thoughts and fight.

Something so profound, so deep within her exclaimed in a soft way that, "It is not over and you are worthy!" These were words she wasn't familiar with but she wanted to believe. From the outside, one might assume that this was a terrible situation. Not Myra, she knew better. She knew that God heard her pray and was delivering just what she has asked for, a life full of hope and health, no matter where her physical body rested. A miracle was in motion.

To Myra, it was never really about her. Helping others to heal was always her greatest desire. But how could she help others when she was in such great need? Not knowing the answers or how they would come about, she was determined to do it. It was her life's purpose and she would fulfill it. Some day, some way, some how.

Myra smiles at her soul. She is not as she was before. She is proud of her hard work and diligence. She is strong and holds beauty and wisdom that were caused by turmoil. "It wasn't all for nothing," she says aloud. The fight was worth it. Myra was worth it. And it has become Myra's greatest aspiration to share with the world that they too are worthy. What does your mirror record sound like? Dare to listen.

Excerpt from Hidden Treasure

…She had been driving and felt an urge to take a left on what seemed to be a deserted dusty road. Rose was listening intuitively to her inner self and obeyed. She drove until her trusty old truck suddenly went dead. Minutes before there wasn't a cloud in the sky but now rain was falling hard. Instead of panicking she knew that everything was working out for her. The deserted road, broken down truck, and heavy rain were exactly what she needed to lead her to discover whatever answers she was looking for. She knew she had to get out of her truck and walk.

There was a forest in sight and she headed in its direction. Soon she saw a small wooden cabin. She was drenched from the rain and needed somewhere to stay dry while she contemplated her next move. As the door creaked open she was surprised to find only an old trunk. She eagerly approached it, pulled on the lock, it opened, and she reached in and pulled out a picture of her future self. She was astonished and felt a wave of emotions so strong that she almost fainted. Her body was warm and her heartbeat became slow. It was as if time stood still. She just stared at this image. Everything she had dreamed about as a child was captured in this picture. She finally started to believe that dreams come true…

Several years after Misty was released from prison, we were in close correspondence. In fact, my husband and I had been witnesses on the happy occasion of her marriage to Matt in 2014. While I was working on the Pen Pal section of Prison Wisdom, *I asked Misty to write an account of her experience taking my LifeStories class at FCI, back in 2010. This is her essay in response.*

Before entering FCI, Tallahassee I had served three years in a county jail, awaiting sentencing. After being in a federal facility two and a half years I signed up for a writing class with Katya Taylor. I had worked hard on "bettering" myself and thought this would be a great opportunity.

My first class just so happened to be on my 30th birthday. I was entering a new decade and phase of my life. I walked in the door and saw desks in a circle, chose the spot that suited me and sat down. A lady with dark hair and warm skin sat to my left with a vase of violet flowers in front of her. Her eyes twinkled as if to say, "Welcome, you are accepted." I knew I was in the right place.

Some of the women in the group were friends and associates that I had spent special moments with. The other ladies I had passed as we went about our daily routines within the prison walls.

Through sharing, I learned many things about myself and my peers. We each began to open up and share our deepest selves. I felt their pains and joys. Through the course of the class I witnessed the ladies, including myself, blossom. There was one special lady that caught my attention and shortly after the class I became her mentor. I was there as she expressed herself and I watched her gain self-love and confidence.

I also went on to instruct the classmates in another writing class after the eight weeks with Katya were over. I knew we all still had more healing and expressions to share. I wasn't going to let my lack of confidence get in the way of helping others and myself.

I have always found writing to be therapeutic. I have written in a journal most of my life. I had written to express joy and pain, but for my eyes only. In the writing class I learned to write using haiku, seed phrases, clusters, and various techniques and styles. I gained so much confidence in myself. Now I write haiku to capture special moments almost daily. I have written multiple 700 words stories and as usual I write in my journal.

I have been out of prison for almost three years now and I write every day. I have gotten married and my husband and I have our own "Happiness Journal" that we write in together to remember how blessed we are. I have plans to write books and speeches. My writing has improved and since I use words to reach and connect with people this has definitely made a big difference. I also plan to do writing classes to assist others in healing and identifying with their true selves like Katya did with me. It helped me and I know it can help others.

The top three things I got from taking this class were more confidence in my writing, new styles and ideas for writing, and most importantly I have a better relationship with myself.

In writing there is power, truth, understanding, and healing. I would advise anyone in prison (physical, mental, emotional, etc.) to take this class. For inmates, this is a beautiful way to express yourself when you live with so many limits. Also, if a person is in prison something led them to make a choice that resulted in a sentence. Writing will assist in healing.

I am so grateful to be a part of Prison Wisdom. Some of my writings have been chosen to share within the pages. To be a part of something so meaningful to myself and others while enlightening and encouraging the world, is truly satisfying.

2015

Leonard Scovens

In order to introduce Leonard, I must first tell you about Agnes Furey. Many years ago I was offering a LifeStories class at a local hospital (for the general public) and Agnes showed up.

When we went around the room introducing ourselves and sharing why we had signed up for the class, Agnes stunned us all when she explained that her daughter and grandson had been murdered, and that she was here to heal -- she hoped writing would help her through her grief.

Her powerful journaling, and the healing it engendered, was a gift to us all. Agnes and I stayed in touch, and she signed up for more of my classes. I learned that she had become interested, and involved, in the restorative justice movement, in which perpetrators and victims came together to heal. She wondered if she could do this with the man who had taken her daughter and grandson's life.

She wrote to Leonard, who was serving a life sentence, and he wrote back. This was the beginning of a long correspondence, which resulted in a remarkable book co-authored by Agnes and Leonard: *Wildflowers in the Median*. Since I had been part of Agnes' journey for a long time, and she knew of my work in the prisons, she asked if I would be willing to write the forward to the book. At that point, I wrote to Leonard. I felt it was important to know who he was before I could begin my essay.

We wrote back and forth, as I worked on my forward, and then continued after the book was published. My correspondence with Leonard could fill its own volume. But for now, let me say that it has been an honor, not only to be part of the healing that has taken place, but to have gained a literary, philosophical, activist pen pal, a man who strives to make a difference with his writing, his leadership, and his struggles to overcome the demons that led to his imprisonment. We have shared that we each have our own prison "ministry," mine from the "outside," his from the "inside."

The following is excerpted from a slightly longer essay.

Chronos

The first few years of my Natural Life Sentence were spent in a daze. How are you supposed to process having to spend the rest of your life in a cage? How does a man's mind make sense of a future of endless captivity? I spent a lot of time ignoring the reality of my situation, stuffing the pain, quelling the madness pumping through my veins. I wandered the prison compound in a tattered blue uniform incessantly smoking hand-rolled cigarettes, hungrily staring at the powder blue sky beyond the fences, so out of touch that at times I'd go for days without so much as putting on deodorant. I didn't belong here. I wanted out. I was a fly in buttermilk and I wanted to stretch my wings and soar. But I was caught and drowning in sludge, the weight of the years ahead dragging me deeper and deeper into my own private lunacy.

I watched the older cons. The guys who'd been in twenty or more years, the survivors. I studied them, fascinating and amazed that they'd made it this far because I knew I wouldn't. I'd cut my own throat before I'd allow my hair to go grey, my sight to dim, and my legs to weaken under the burden of the years.

I watched them thinking they were suckers for giving the State all those dead birthdays. I clocked their movements, trying to decipher their attitudes, attempting to glean wisdom from how they handled themselves, wisdom in how to live through the pain I was burying inside.

I didn't learn much. A lot of those cats were old folks who'd made it by the skin of their teeth. They didn't know anything I didn't know or wouldn't learn on my own. Some, like Pop Gates, did their time by staying drunk or high. Some, like Old Man Curtis, lived in a private world of fantasy and delusion as he picked up discarded cigarette butts off the ground all day and smoked them while talking softly with the Queen of England. Some, like Mao, immersed themselves in the prison lifestyle and didn't care about freedom any more. It didn't exist. They found joy and satisfaction in prison yard drama. And some, like Brother Yusef, moved closer to an understanding of the Most High.

Sitting with Brother Yusef one mid-summer afternoon, both of us relaxing on a mound of grass on the rec yard, staring at the blonde sun smoldering beyond the gates and above the trees of this wilderness that surrounded our cage, I asked him: "Man, how did you do it? How'd you handle the time?"

I wanted him to comfort me. I wanted him to tell me something about how God consoles the wounded and weary, giving them strength to make it through. But he didn't. He just looked at me. In silence. Searching my eyes.

He must have heard the suppressed panic in my voice. He must have seen the turmoil broiling in my heart. The growing rage. He must have seen the desperation etched into the lines of my creased brow and in the permanent frown that was disfiguring my face. He must have seen my agony because he turned away too quickly and sighed as if he had to get loose of the wild emotions he'd touched by staring too deeply into me. After a long quiet moment he finally said, "You just handle it, brother. That's all. You just handle it."

I was staring at his profile. The white sun was glistening on his ebony skin. He was fifty-nine but thirty-four years of incarceration had preserved him. He looked forty, and just then, young enough to be as desperate for freedom as I was.

There was nothing but silence left between us, dangling like a hanged corpse twisting in the wind. There was nothing more he could teach me about dealing with the pain. I stood, staring at him while he dreamed beyond our shared hell, then walked away – time's embrace tightening around me, squeezing the breath from my lungs, breaking my young savage heart.

The following are brief excerpts from some of Leonard's letters to me. They are not in order by date, but rather express recurring themes that define Leonard's sense of self and his life's mission. One day perhaps, a fuller rendering can be made of his writings, but for now, please enter into his consciousness, as he expresses, with ink and paper, his journey of liberation.

Ah, Katya, my life is pretty simple. I have work to do, "promises to keep and miles to go before I sleep." I've subordinated most of the other impulses I have that are natural to a man. My focus is virtually solely committed to succeeding in what I've set out to do. I see life through that lens. Everything I invest my time and energy in must have something to do with that.

This isn't necessarily new. None of it is, really. For ten years, through many twists and turns and advances and setbacks and changes and turnarounds, I've been moving toward accomplishing something with my life. I was not raised to be a killer or drug addict or criminal or convict. In my mid-twenties I began to understand how much of a disappointment I was to the woman who'd raised me to be far more than I'd made of myself. As I matured I began to understand that I had to do, and be, something more.

Life is not linear. So there was no conversion experience for me where I suddenly became angelic and sinless. Over a period of time, though, I have shifted my perspective a bit. I've figured out what works and I'm working it to the best of my ability. And I'm hoping that this will enrich my life, and all those who come near me....

You asked me what writing project I'm working on. I've had a sort of memoir in mind but I set that aside for now... I am working on a sort of daily meditation book. I don't even have a title for it yet, but I have 90 quotes that I'm using. I'll riff on each one for a ninety-day path to healing in the aftermath of trauma. That's the theme. How do we get through the pain after something bad has happened to us? How do we use the pain to grow and transform and become stronger and wiser than we were before we were hurt? I'm designing the book as an answer to these questions....

The thing about fear is that it only has power when you surrender to it. And that is something I do not do. I realize that I've been conditioned to fear abandonment and, as a consequence, intimacy. It's a crazy thing. Because I yearn for intimacy but am terrified on so many levels by the prospect. God forbid I heed that terror. My life is rich because of the amount of intimacy I enjoy with those I adore. Were I a coward my life would be miserable, barren, poor.

But look, I've a new friend I bare my heart to and she doesn't throw it in my face and break it. Instead, she sends me poetry and lovely thoughts and invites me to come outside and play awhile in the sunshine with her where it's warm. I've absolutely no intention of denying myself the joy of hanging out with you.

I want to share the sunset with you. I'm watching it through my window as a cool silk breeze slips across my skin. The sun is orange – a little ball of orange fire in the sky, and it is just beginning to descend beneath the point where it burns the clouds in front of it mauve and violet.

The sky is clear but for a scattering of clouds, their bellies orange now, their interiors pale purple. A beautiful scene. I'm blessed to be able to view it right now.

I have been living with your letter. Please forgive me for taking so much time in responding in full. It certainly is not because I've forgotten, or I don't know, set it aside. What's the phrase I'm looking for?

Suffice it to say that I've kept your words and thoughts near me, have given them space to roam in the gardens of my heart and mind. Actually spending time with them allows me a more nuanced response than if I just toss you the initial sparks rather than share with you the full flame.

Your *Mirrors* poem, this off the cuff "freestyle," if you will, has some really wonderful language and ideas in it:

Mirrors, like a pond so still
like a cloud ever moving
like a face you wish you could know
if only, if only
being human weren't such a puzzle
Let the mirror guide you
through the wilderness
showing you the answer as you
cry out your predicament
the oracle incarnate
so clear, like ice before it breaks...

The last line, I really love that!

I'm in a period of transition, Katya. I am looking at the waters and am no longer tricked by the surface. It is my duty at this point to enter it, to go into it, travel deeper, to break the surface, to travel through the image into the interior to find whatever it is that has been waiting for me there.

Mirrors. Water and mirrors. And images. Reflections and journeys into the depths of Psyche...

This "list poem" is in response to a seed phrase I sent Leonard: "Things I love"

Things I Love

A letter from someone whose mind I enjoy

Miles Davis making magic in Kind of Blue

Anything John Coltrane

Blueberry muffins, blueberry pie, blueberry anything

Sweet, rich scents –sandalwood incense, fresh pine, autumn leaves

Earth colors – the colors of leaves and earth in autumn

A poem that knocks me flat

Sylvia Plath and Anne Sexton

Lust for me in a woman's eyes

An underdog

The downtrodden, the transcendent

Success

Anything done well and with skill

My nephew's smile, my niece's laughter, my sister's voice

Anything Jill Scott sings

Anything Nina Simone sings

Anything Joni Mitchell sings

Anything the woman I love sings

Love

The moon

Making love with the window open when it's raining

The colors you choose when addressing letters to me in crayon.

I've been trying write about my prison experience for some time, but really couldn't figure out a way to do it that would be functional. I mean, it's relatively simple to keep a plot going when you have characters moving from place to place doing this or that. But most of my prison time has been done in confinement. So the question for me was how to write about those experiences, about relationships conducted through the mail, about spiritual and psychological dramas in a way that was gripping and compelling.

And I needed a sort of climax. I'd wanted it to be something good, you know. So that it could be a sort of coming of age success story in its own weird way. Which is part of why I kept putting the writing off. Because I was still living the story that needed to be written.

Now, however, I have all the material that I need. And I've largely figured out how to write it in a way that could grip and entertain an audience. Or they will most definitely learn something. And if I do my job right one will not be able to come away from the story unmoved. I do, however, believe that a writer must grip and entertain an audience first and foremost. Then slip in the good stuff.

At any rate, I'm playing with titles right now. *Sorrow's Light...?*

The following excerpt is from 2013.

Yes, I am indeed 37. I will be 38 on August 3. And yes, we are timeless in that we connect as Souls who do not place much significance on the chains Chronos attaches to our bodies. Our souls have been here (wherever here is) from the dawn and will be here for many more forevers. Kindred spirits? Yes. Indeed.

I love your view on our overall interconnectedness, as human beings. I agree that we are *all* a family, a tribe, a community, an interconnected gene pool, as you say, spinning on this pretty little green and blue planet trying to figure it all out. And we murder our brothers and sisters because so many of us are lost and groping in the dark, manifesting the worst of what we are capable of rather than the best...

Tribulation

Be bold, hold the line.
Keep the wolves at bay with smiles
and laughter with peace signs painted
on steel bars in blood and love spelled
out on stone floors with tears.

"There is no progress without struggle,"
says the snail, "and pieces of yourself
marking the slow slog over rough terrain. "

So delight in the punch that comes
when you stand up and stare down the bully
who feeds on fear and is conquered
by faith; count it all joy
and write another poem, sing a new song,
believe with urgency.

This is how we will win:
After the stitches have been removed
and the rage has been transformed
into wisdom – we will, in defiance,
resume teaching that love is subversion
and, thus, worthy of praise.

One thing I find interesting is that everyone in this environment expects me to be emotionless, somehow and…I don't know. I was once cold, numb and broken. But I am whole now and I live with my heart open. I mean, I'm a big guy and I look mean, I guess, but I'm living with my heart right there on the line, and it hurts like hell when it gets stepped on. I know I'm tough and can make it through anything. Knowing that gives me a little freedom to feel deeply, to live with this wide open heart, to put myself out there…

I haven't put pen to paper for any reason for about two weeks. I've been engaged in a daily fight to renew my mind and revitalize my spirit. I've been walking around the same mountain for too long now, and I've decided to put my back to it. I declare myself healed, strengthened, blessed and moving forward into my greater destiny.

This time in my life is about growth, transformation, the removal of strongholds, chain-breaking -- learning humility, patience, gaining strength, wisdom, depth. This has been a tough, humbling and sometimes humiliating experience, but I am learning and I will be empowered on the other side of this...

I enjoyed an extensive yoga session outside today. It was such a gorgeous day. The blue sky was filled with bundles of fluffy clouds and the sun was shining. I was barefoot in a field of little white and purple wildflowers. During the headstand I watched honey bees gathering pollen at eye level against that beautiful sky. It was awesome. So peaceful, and the earth smelled sweet...

As I look back over the years and try to account for the things that have wrought dramatic changes in me, I've got to hold yoga responsible for much of it. Yoga, tai chi, meditation and study – all have served as a foundation as I explored the ideas Agnes and I were working with. I was a mess for most of my life. It has taken me years of some very hard work to undo a lot of damage and to begin to heal and to change and to grow beyond the psychoses I inherited. Here I stand new. A witness, a survivor whose debt to this planet is beyond measure.

Hmm... I don't think you necessarily idealize reality when you say that we operate as pure *consciousness*, and so transcend the delusion of appearances. Whether it is the peal of a taxi's horn, the gentle sound of rain falling against a roof, the sound of 84 men talking at once or the crash of thunder – we can connect to our Selves, the Source, one another. We can connect to Consciousness. It's true. I can dig that...

I Remember A Room

I remember a room as cold as the coldest night of a hard, cold New York winter. I was nude except for a square of cream-colored fabric I wore around my waist like a towel. I was colder than I could remember ever being. Even that night about twenty years earlier that I stood at a bus stop in Baltimore City, from 11 pm until 3 a.m. shivering in a windbreaker while the early winter breeze cut through to bone and marrow. I cried that night, I was so cold, and prayed to God that he'd make that damned bus come and release me from purgatory.

It was colder in that cell though. And I didn't cry. I pulled the plastic covered mattress over my body and curled beneath it. The floor was a slab of ice. My body wouldn't stop trembling, the stitches in the cut on my forearm tore from my moving the mattress this way and that over my body, and I began to bleed again, which prompted the guards to take the mattress. Then there was nothing but cold. It wrapped itself around me and smiled a victorious smile that sapped me of pride, strength, will and tears. So cold.

After writing on this first (I remember a room) seed prompt, Leonard shared his feelings about writing for an "assignment." On the following pages, he responds to several more prompts.

So, there you go, that was cool. I generally don't like prompts. I'm a free verse rather than sonnet kind of cat. Whimsical. Meaning, I like to chase my own series of shadows. And I'm a rebel to boot. Which means following someone's directions and such doesn't naturally appeal to me. But your mind and spirit appeal to me. And your prompts obviously mean something to you. So I'll take a little prompting from you every now and then, because that's what friends do. Right??

My Heart Leaps Up When

My heart leaps up when I imagine what it will feel like to finally finish one of my long running writing projects. There is the Higher Ground Facilitation Manual, which has been in one form of disarray or another for two years. And there is X, which I'm probably renaming again to City of Tears, and which has been calling me daily, for a week. I have refused to heed the call however. What is it…fear? Of what? Of failure? Of success? Oh hogwash. I don't think it's fear of anything. I imagine it's just stone cold laziness. My old friend procrastination. You know you gotta do something and should be doing that something rather than merely contemplating doing it, and end up doing everything but that something you know you should be doing! So rather than write on City of Tears, I'll read the Great Controversy, and pretend it's work.

My heart leaps up when I imagine the sense of accomplishment I'll feel to have finally finished the job, to be able to breathe and get the babe ready to meet the world. My heart leaps up when I imagine being justified as an artist.

My Hands

My hands are hard, fragile things. They have been broken by walls, have wiped tears away, have held baby birds in their palms and saved them from death. They have cleaned blood from new wounds and have opened wounds. They are scarred, their knuckles padded with dark hardened flesh and knotted with old scar tissue. These calloused hands have reached into earth and love, have unkinked knots in tight bodies, have been held between small palms and kissed. Tears have fallen on these brown hands. My own and others. These hands have held one million pens and have written more words than can fill a sky, words that have become poems and letters, confessions of love, essays, sentences, novels and paragraphs pulled from a heart as fragile and open as these scarred, arthritic hands.

Why I Write

I write because if I didn't I'd grab a fresh razor
and call it a day.

I write because dreams live first through language.

I write around tall corners and unravel darkness in ink
because pens were made for love.

I write to overcome my fear of gravity.

I write because it tastes like joy.

> *Now, Leonard's letter excerpts continue.*

I am running after a deeper, more soulful connection to the Most High. When I find happiness I hold on to it, and drink it to the dregs or to the lees. But my wound won't heal and I am cool with that. There is a very deep sadness that those of us who have done the irrevocable wrong must cling to, in my opinion. Because we must be reminded daily what we owe.

As I move forward in my life, Katya, it increasingly becomes about what I must give. From the soul. And that doesn't mean that I feel I must whip myself or punish and diminish myself. It just means that to whom much is given, much is required... Here I am. Weathered, perhaps, but whole and completely human and alive.

I'm done feeling sorry for myself. I am done with shame. I will be who I am, I accept my reality in full with a clean, hard eye on what I will do to *shape* it, to mold it, to make from the rough materials I've been given in this life something wondrous and beautiful. But not only that, I intend to change this world. We are spit onto the planet and have a finite amount of time along with an infinite amount of possibility to add to the knowledge of humanity...

Something that has been on my mind and heart recently, and that is working itself through my life. Let me put it like this. I'm beginning to reawaken to myself as an artist, a writer. I set so much of that aside when I chose to focus my attention on Restorative Justice, Higher Ground, and teaching. When I decided in 2011 that I was going to focus on these things, I turned away from focusing on my development as an artist, writer and poet. My work became about function, purpose and content, rather than on form, artistry, the development of my psyche and craft...

Reading the Plath *(the poet Sylvia Plath)* biography is reminding me of what it has truly been about for me. I'd forgotten my place in the scheme of things. I've invested an enormous amount of my consciousness and identity on how I've been received by guards, prisoners and others who make up the dysfunctional community I live in. I've been banging my head against the limitations, preconceptions, misconceptions and prejudices of this population... What I really want to do is create a body of work insightful and powerful enough to create changes in the system...

Here the cranes seem to be in the midst of mating season. There are between 15 and 20 maroon domed cranes that hang out in this compound during the day. Beautiful, gangly creatures, these.

There's one tall slender crane with yellow eyes that I'm bonding with. I hold out my hand with a piece of bread in it and he will walk right up to me with his knock-kneed walk and gently snatch it from my palm with his beak. Several of them will do this. There's a certain amount of trust between convicts and cranes. There is a poem in there somewhere....

Have you ever seen them fly? They look like Olympic swimmers doing the breaststroke across the sky...

Have you been entertained? Intrigued? Have I been able to inspire any thought or emotion that wasn't in the picture before you opened the envelope, took these pages in hand, and began to read my words?

I wonder where you are today as you read this letter. I dig the fact that I'm time traveling with you. And that my now is merging with your now at this very moment, in this very instant. So, in a very real way, I am here with you and I wonder if you can feel my soul.

I am fire. *(Leonard is astrologically a Leo.)* I cast light, heat. I warm to the bone, to the essence, to the core, and I wonder if you can feel that. I imagine that you do. And, while I realize that may be vanity, I amuse myself by thinking that it is one of the reasons you seem to be enjoying our correspondence.

Because I feel *you*. It stands to reason that if I can feel your energy coming through to me, like sky blue and electricity, or sky blue electricity…then you can feel *me*.

I'm trying to find the words here to capture this wild idea that souls are not bound by time or flesh or the illusion of distance.

And I'll leave it at that.

Leonard's Wheel Pose

Post note:

It has now been ten years since Agnes and Leonard have been writing one another, bonding in their desire to create ways for restorative justice to find a place in the prison system. Leonard has created a template for a group process he calls the Higher Ground Workshop Series. These groups are meant to be peer-facilitated, and help inmates heal and become self-empowered, nurturing a sense of empathy, for self, fellow inmates, their families and communities. He has put together a group instruction manual, and more recently a facilitator's manual for those who would be leading groups within the prisons.

Agnes has posted and continues to update an Achieve Higher Ground Facebook page. AHG's vision is "a criminal justice system that pursues healing and restorative outcomes as fervently as it presently pursues punishment and revenge-based outcomes."

At the end of our discussion, Agnes felt it was important to add the following words.

"All of us in prison and out deserve hope. The reality we lose sight of is that most people in prisons will return home to live with us. And in all my time volunteering in the prisons, I have never met a person who deserves to be thrown away...."

Dispatch from Confinement

"I was once lost, but now I'm found. I was a mixed up, banged up, misguided youth who did a terrible thing I will spend the rest of my life atoning for. I spent many years in prison messed up, mad…but the light of love, forgiveness, accountability and reconciliation inspired me to put in some real Soul work and heal. Agnes touched me, inspired me, and changed my life with the light that shone through her soul and acts of mercy. I am testimony to her work and to the truth and power of her philosophy. I am testimony to how the most wretched of human beings can grow, change and become renewed… I will touch whomever I can. I will delight myself with acts of revolutionary random kindness while inspiring riots of peace and reconciliation…"

Martin Rivers

This is how I first met Martin (Marty) Rivers. Since I had been teaching for a long time in the prison system, my name somehow found its way to an organization that helps prisoners distribute their art: Safe Streets Arts Foundation. In 2012, soon after Thanksgiving, I received an email from the organization asking if I would be willing to write inmates a holiday greeting card. They would send me a list of ten individuals who might not have the support system that would include receiving personal mail over the holidays. I said yes. For one thing, I'm a writer, and enjoy writing letters (real letters as well as email); for another, due to my experience offering writing to inmates, I feel a kindred connection to people who have been incarcerated and who have been all but forgotten by the society at large ("Out of sight and mind" as one of our anthologies was titled.)

I received the list (all men) and sent a hand-written card to each. Several of the men wrote back. Of these, Marty and I closely connected and have continued writing and sharing our life stories ever since. When I first viewed his art, I found it hard to believe that solely with ink pens he was able to produce this kind of work. I was stunned to discover that he had been in solitary for *years on end* (ten, in all, as it turned out) and that while in such isolation, he'd managed not only to stay sane but to enlist in his own evolution by enrolling in a large number of correspondence courses (a list is given within the body of his letters). That Marty is now "in general population" and has a good chance, because of his determination and spirit, to be granted parole, makes me very happy. I hope that he will share his talents as a stonemason and as an artist to benefit society—and himself, as a man who has earned his freedom.

Marty as a young boy

Marty writes.

"I was a good kid and everyone called me Little Marty. That was before I grew into a 6'3" giant! I wanted to share with you the little boy that I was."

Dear Mrs. Katya Taylor,

First and foremost let me take this opportunity to extend my sincere regards to you and your family, and truly hope that when you receive this letter it finds you in the greatest of health and in the highest of spirits.

On 12/14/12 I received your correspondence/greeting card along with the photocopied prisoner resource printout you included. Thank you.

Mrs. Taylor, to say I was surprised to hear from you would be an understatement and truly am grateful you took the time to write me and express kind words.

I do not receive greeting cards very often, especially from individuals I do not know, and am humbled in many aspects by your kindness. It's not common these days that people have the time to extend a small act that means a lot to someone such as myself, who is incarcerated….

Your kind words and the gesture itself put a smile on my face, which is rare and far between…

Sincerely,
Marty

Dec 21, the Winter Solstice

Hi Martin –what a nice surprise finding your letter in my mailbox. Because of e-mail, it is a rare moment when a "real letter" arrives through the post office. Your handwriting is so elegant, as if you have studied calligraphy. Have you??

The organization that sent the newsletter (enclosed in my envelope) gave me ten addresses of inmates around America, and you happened to be one of the ten. So far you are the only one who has responded... and with your own home made envelope!

I have enclosed one if you feel like writing back to me again.

Martin, I grew up in California, in San Francisco, and I have been through Crescent City, I'm sure. Are you from California originally or is that the facility you were sent to from somewhere else?

If you like, we can share something of our lives with one another. One can never have too many pen pals, I find.

Today is a special day for me, because 25 years ago my daughter (my one and only child) was born on the Solstice. She just graduated with her masters in architecture and has found a job with a local firm and thus only lives 2 miles away, lucky us. Tom and I have lived in Tallahassee for 22 years, and feel happy and settled here. Have you ever been to Florida? We are way up north, near the Georgia border, in the Panhandle. Unlike South Florida, we have some manner of seasons, many kinds of trees, live oak, as well as palm, and pine, and a few rolling hills. This is the capital city, as you probably know.

How old are you, Martin?? Is Pelican Bay a place where you can take classes, learn things, create things, work out, or is it more limited in programs? The reason I ask is because I teach creative writing in my local (women's) prison, and we are allowed to publish the student writing in an anthology at the end of each course. It is so special to write with my students, and to "become one" as we share the stories, fact and fictional, that emerge from our pens and imagination.

As for me, when I'm not teaching writing, I'm in my garden, growing veggies, herbs, flowers, and fruit trees; I'm cooking vegetarian (plus fish) meals, I'm reading many books from our public library, compiling books of my own writings, walking, dancing, and going to visit St. George island, a beautiful beach two hours away.

Do you ever draw with colored pencils, or have other art materials available? It really helps me when I am being creative, and exercising my body too (walking, dancing, yoga)... Do they have a basketball court at Pelican Bay???

Now, please let me hear from you. What do you love to do, what are your hopes and dreams?? What music do you like to listen to?? Fill in the blanks, whatever comes to mind that you'd like to share.

From later letters.

Dear Katya,

Be sure to send some postcards of your travels in July when you go to celebrate your 50th year of friendship with your college roommate. The Finger Lakes sound like a beautiful area! I wish that I could go someplace serene and peaceful. I need a vacation! This place can drive a person nuts, the prison atmosphere itself, as well that it's death row. The entire appeals process, and guys getting executed every two to three months (ever since Sept 2011) lays so heavy and is so stressful. It's difficult keeping it together!

In my understanding, Marty was not on death row – so I'm not sure why he was housed there.

I too wish you had a magic wand that you could wave to bring me some measure of peace – and poof! I'll be somewhere other than this place, somewhere living a peaceful life... I'd love to be home with Mom and Dad, helping them around the house and with all their gardening (flowers and vegetable gardens)!

You mentioned that my art looks like photographs. Thank you. Most of my drawings come from pages out of magazines. My specialty is women. I can draw them like there is no tomorrow. However, I can draw pretty much anything. Animals are hard because it's hard to draw fur. Especially with a standard ink pen.

Anyways, you stated you wish to help support my art and my creative side. I am humbled Katya. Your letters, your kind words of encouragement have done that. Your impact on my life has been huge. You have given me hope and something to look forward to. I know we have only known each other for a short time and you have treated me with kindness, more acts of kindness than my own family. I am so grateful for that and cannot even begin to put it into words. I am honored to be in your life and inspired by your presence. You truly are a unique and beautiful woman and I have a special place in my heart for you and your family. All I can say is thank you.

Well, I have been busy. I just finished my communications course and am waiting on my certificate now and my new course material. I am eligible in the fall to start actual college courses and start on my AA degree. I am still doing my other studies as well, and am thinking about taking some parenting classes. I don't have any kids but I think it would be beneficial.

I asked Marty to tell me about some of the courses he has taken (and received certificates for). He sent me a list. The following six correspondence classes took about ten months or so to finish.

1) The Way to Happiness

2) Understanding and Handling Addiction

3) The Conditions of Life

4) Personal Integrity

5) Handling Suppression

6) Effective Communication

1) Glaucoma
2) The Human Eye
3) Self Esteem and Adjusting to Blindness
4) Independent Living
5) Diabetes
6) Self Help Groups

Pre-Release Journaling Project (required for release).

1) Family and other Relationships
2) Anger
3) Thinking Errors
4) Relapse Prevention
5) My Change Plan
6) Employment Skills
7) Life Management
8) Coping Skills
9) Values

The Ratha Foundation teaches meditation courses, each one involving a year of study.

1) The Myth of Freedom
2) Turning the Mind into an Ally
3) The Power of Patience: Healing Anger

Prisoner Express is an organization offered by Cornell University to promote and advocate for inmates.

1) Basic Human Anatomy and Physiology (one of five inmates to actually finish the course)
2) Western Civilization
3) Astronomy

> Marty completed the Alcoholics Anonymous course as well and took Bible study courses from various churches, about 10 certificates, including courses offered by prison.
>
> Finally, he earned his own G.E.D.
>
> Marty added.

"You must understand that I did all of these courses within the last five years, taking two or three at a time."

One example of an earned certificate

These Welfare/Security Checks are to take place every 30 minutes 24/7. The memo sent to staff stipulates that they are to wake us up if they cannot see us, or if they don't see us breathing. So in the middle of the night they come in 15 or 16 times to do these checks. You are going to be woken up regardless,

In addition, this program has had an adverse impact on inmates currently housed in S.H.U. The program has caused sleep deprivation, denial/delay to medical treatment, law library access, exercise (yard), showers, canteen, packages, visits and our meals. Sleep deprivation is cruel and unusual punishment, a direct violation of our 8th amendment. Medical, Law Library and Yard are a direct violation of a Federal Court order.

After receiving this information from Marty, I wrote to the governor and warden, and whether my letter made any difference, I don't know.

But this practice was rescinded... for the time being.

Marty sent a drawing to my husband Tom. Here is his explanation about it:

By now, you should have received the drawing I sent Tom. That truck was the first one I ever drew, so it has a special meaning to me. And I wanted to give it to Tom for Father's Day. I know he was probably not expecting anything from me, but he sure has been a good father to Alana and a good husband to you. So it is my way of showing him that I respect him as a man, husband and as a father. I hope he enjoys it.

As for how long it took me to draw it? That one drawing took me about sixteen hours. Depending on the drawing it could have been longer. But I did it in two and a half days, which was about 16 hours.

I started to draw in 2009, out of need, as I don't get any money from my family. So in order to get soap, toothpaste, deodorant, shampoo, etc. I started to draw. I would do a birthday card or drawing for someone in exchange for some hygiene. Basically a hustle to meet my needs.

Come to find out I am actually fairly good at it and it serves a purpose.

Since I acquired this talent, I have also used it as a tool to give back. I have donated artwork to various organizations to help fund educational programs for poor families and prisoners. I donated big art pieces to Cornell University and the archdiocese of Los Angeles and have probably given away at least fifty pieces of art.

My artwork consists of sexy women (big hit within prison), Native American art, Mexican culture, demons, fantasy, etc., and I can do portraits as well. Most of my creations come from pictures out of magazines. Basically if I have a photo of something, I can draw it.

Marty's "Father's Day" gift to Tom

It took sixteen hours to draw it.

As for questions about nature, well I have not seen a tree, flower, leaf or a bug in almost ten years. I have not seen daylight in six years and three months. So my memory of these things has faded.

The prison put a channel on TV that only plays the radio. So it was the first time I heard music in a while and let me tell you, I was dancing in my cell. It felt really good to hear music. It definitely made my day.

In my spare time I help guys with legal cases. I am what you would consider a jail-house lawyer. I know the law very well. It kind of comes easy for me, and actually I wanted to study business law. It's something that has always interested me.

In addition I help others who are studying to get their GED. It's amazing how many men in prison don't have a GED or even a 9th grade education. It's even more rare for those who actually care to get a GED.

When I am not drawing or helping someone, I tend to do a lot of reading. Both fiction and non-fiction. I just finished reading "Cognition of Intelligence," identifying the mechanisms of the mind. Prior to that I just read an introduction to photography. It was a college textbook someone gave me.

I have probably read 2,000 books since my incarceration.

I am currently reading a book on how to speak Italian. Why? Well, I am half Italian, a quarter Mexican and a quarter Native American. My mom is Italian…well her grandpa, my great grandfather came to the US in 1906 by way of Ellis Island.

I have been doing research on my family history, specifically my mom's dad's side of the family. My grandfather who passed away in 1993 served in WW II.

You know I have taken many steps to ensure that I am somehow successful in my life. And to do that is very hard from behind these walls. I have struggled in many aspects of my life, battling drug addiction, anger, etc. It's a difficult thing to be honest with yourself and to reflect on what needs to change. We can all sit here and say we did this or that, but true change shines through your actions in your attitude. And I am glad you were able to see it…

In regards to me helping others, well, in prison you would be surprised at how many people don't want help. One out of a hundred, maybe. And as long as I can help that one it's a start.

You asked about me not talking to my family on the phone? We are not allowed phone calls in an isolation unit. We have no phones or windows and are locked in our cells for 22 ½ hours a day. So my only communication is through letters. If I get out of S.H.U I could use the phone… maybe one day.

I continue to work out on a daily basis. A strong mind and a strong body go hand in hand. I am in great shape. It's something I put a lot of effort into. It's a way to release my frustration in a manner that's constructive rather than destructive.

Thank you for recognizing my strengths, and all that I have done. It was not easy to travel this path, and it has broken many people. I am fortunate enough to be mentally capable of overcoming the hardships I have had to face. It has made me stronger and a better man.

As for my artistic talents? Well, I was able to find solace in it. It is my form of meditation.

You inquired about how much time I'm serving. I'm currently serving 15 years to life. Basically a life sentence. If I stay out of trouble, I do have a chance for parole in 2018. But yes, I'm doing life.

You mentioned in your letter that I am an inspiration to you. Wow, I am humbled. However I would say you're my inspiration. I understand that I have endured hardships over the last decade. I never broke a rule and I had everything taken from me. I'm just one of thousands who have been subjected to these tactics.

The physical aspect of being locked up is probably the easiest part of doing time. The mental aspect of being deprived of human contact, sunlight, etc. is hard and gets harder as time goes on. Many people fail to grasp the true impact of extreme isolation. It's not a tool to rehabilitate but designed to mentally break a person. Those of us who endure are allowed a greater appreciation for life, the opportunities we are afforded and time to reflect on our mistakes.

Unfortunately everything comes with a price. To say this has not affected me would be a lie. It has been taxing in many aspects, both mentally and physically.

The reason I say you are my inspiration? Well, it's because of individuals like you who look past our mistakes and look at our potential, treat us as human beings and believe that change is possible through education, encouragement, positive thinking, and integrity. Those of us who have suffered look to people like you and see that humanity has not forgotten us, which in turn fuels us to fight for reform in how the system operates.

The alternative is to be broken, and that's not an option. It's not in me to give up. So thank you for believing in me.

Your mom was right about education. Through education doors break down the barrier of ignorance. However, it's up to the individual to put that knowledge into use.

We must strive for a better quality of life not only for ourselves but for those around us. I know that a lot of people are self-serving and only care about what's in it for them. You see a lot of that here in prison.

Education will only take you so far. One must then look within the heart and reflect on compassion, love, trust, kindness, honesty, loyalty, personal integrity, and most of all the needs of others.

I don't claim to be an angel. I have done many bad things in my life and caused pain to others. I take full responsibility for this, and deeply regret. We all have our demons, but it's what we learn from our experiences that define who we are. And the ones who rise above stand out in many ways.

I know there are a lot of people who view me as a criminal, etc. And in a way I am. But I am the exception to that view. I could have made the decision to continue to be an idiot. But I chose to step up to the plate and show these people I am not a criminal, and was just messed up on drugs and misguided.

I chose to address my demons (drug addiction) head on. I took the hard road that very few people in prison actually take, and that's being honest with ones self and doing what's necessary to bring about positive change. It's not easy to do that. I just did not want to die in a prison cell without having accomplished something. Whether it was educating myself or helping others, doing it in a way that shows there is a life outside these walls, and that even though I am behind these walls, change is possible.

My normal day consists of the following: Wake up at 4:00 a.m., wash up, clean the cell, drink a cup of coffee, use restroom. At 4:30 working out for one hour and a half. 6:00, shower in the sink, wash the cell, do laundry, read, draw, write. Eat lunch around 1:00 pm, read, watch TV, go to yard, eat dinner around 5:00 pm, watch TV or draw or read, go to sleep at 9:00 pm. And do it all over again for years on end. I spend 22 ½ hours in a cell (8 by 10 feet).

I try to stay busy.

Marty's work out schedule

Here's a list of what I do per week...

NOTE: Keep in mind EACH workout is a half day.

MON
(25) 22 Count Burpias
(5) push ups (5) Kicks
25) Brown Eagles
(25) 18 Count Burpies
4 push ups 4 Kicks
25) Brown Eagles
(25) 14 Count Burpies
3 push up 3 Kicks
(25) Brown Eagles
(25) Navy SEAL Burpies
(25) Brown Eagles
(25) 10 Count Burpees
2 push ups 2 Kicks
(25) Brown/ Eagles
(25) 8 Count Burpies
2 push ups
(25) Brown Eagles
(100) Navy SEAL Burpies

TUES
(50) Push ups
(50) Dips
(50) Curls / 25 each arm
(50) Backarms
(50) Shoulder presses
(50) Lawn Mower pulls 25/each arm
(50) Wide push ups
(50) Dips
(50) Curls "
(50) Backarms
Pull ups
87654321 in the front
12345678
Reverse pull ups
87654321
12345678
In close pull ups (front)
87654321
12345678
Behind the neck pull ups
87654321
12345678

WED
(100) Squats
(100) Lunges
(100) Hotbox steps
(100) Calf Raises
(100) Squat Kicks
(100) Hamstrings
(100) Bouree Squats
(100) Reverse Lunges
(100) Mountain Climbers
(100) Jump Squats 4 sets of (25)
(750) Crunches
(250) Full Sit ups.

Written out for me in a letter – see the prison censor stamp

311

Katya, last week I got some really unexpected news from the two organizations I donate some of my artwork to. Cornell University's Art Director sent me a printout off the internet of the Philadelphia Art Exhibit at City Hall last year, where a few select pieces of art (mine being one) were shown.

I got to see a couple of my drawings. To my understanding it was a real success and my works got a lot of praise.

In addition, I donated some artwork to legal services for prisoners with children. They are based here in California. They bring awareness about isolation, and S.H.U. conditions. Anyway, I donated a handful of pieces and my work was showcased at this exhibit.

They sent me about ten letters from people who attended the exhibit and wrote me about how much they enjoyed my artwork, and stated that they hear our cries for reform.

To say the least, it was a pretty awesome feeling. I was glad so many people thought my art was good. However, I was surprised by how many people are on our side to end long term solitary confinement.

I submitted my application for college enrollment and have to get approved. If I do, I will be the first person in my family to go to college. In 2008 I was the first boy in my family to finish high school.

You inquired about how I created the roses. Well, it was no simple task.

As you know I have not seen flowers in a very long time, or any nature: trees, flowers, etc. except in books or magazines.

So, I saw a magazine that had a shampoo ad and it had a small picture of a rose next to it. It was no bigger than your fingernail. There was not a lot of detail because it was so small.

I used that idea as an idea and foundation on how I should form the concept of a rose. So with that in mind I just tried until I got the image I had in my head. Hence, my version of a rose.

The rest was basic shading with black and red ink pens. It took me about a week to do your card. And I felt it came out fairly good considering I did not have a pattern of a rose. As long as you liked it, I am happy.

In regards to your mom being named Rose? I was actually going to draw a different flower but when I saw the rose I had an urge to make you a rose. So maybe it was fate. And I sense your mom was just as beautiful as her name.

Marty's "Rose" birthday card for me, as described in his letter.

Katya, you stated you were surprised at how I create artwork using only ink pens. Well lots of time and practice have afforded me the opportunity to refine artistic skills. I am what you call a "self taught" artist. I have never had any formal training or been educated in the technique of drawing.

My skills have basically come from trial and error. You must understand that my only medium of drawing is with ink pens. That's due to my circumstances. Drawing with an ink pen is very difficult. One slip of the pen and that's it, your whole drawing is ruined. So you have to be OCD when you draw like this!

The first step in learning how to draw is "gradation." This is the process of shading light to dark or dark to light. This is what gives the drawing depth and makes the image look real.

Then it comes to finding something that you like and want to draw. You can do this by tracing or sketching out a pattern.

Many of my drawings take hours on end. And being that I'm stuck in my cell 22 ½ hours a day, I have hours to spare.

I draw only in my cell on a concrete slab that forms my desk. That is where I write, draw, sketch, on that desk. However, if I am doing a large drawing (two pages) then I will use the bunk as my drawing table.

As for custody staff viewing my work? None of these guys care to interact with me or anyone else. They are taught to dislike us. And not to trust or befriend us in any way. So the only ones who see my drawings are the people I send them to.

After more than ten years in solitary, Marty finally was able (in 2015) to move into general population, and into a different prison. It was an enormous change from being with just a few men in the isolation cells to being surrounded by as many as 500 other inmates. Finally, after more than three years of corresponding, we were able to talk on the phone.

I just wanted to say how good it is to be able to talk to you and to hear your voice. I am so happy and just wish I could talk to you longer and truly share some of my thoughts with you. As you know I am very good at writing letters. I just would like to be able to hold a good conversation like a normal person.

I still get up at 4:00 am and work out, and will probably do that until the day I die. It's been such a big part of my life all these years. It doesn't seem normal if I change.

We walk to breakfast. Yes, I said walk! Which is crazy, because I haven't walked to chow since 1999. So it takes some getting used to being around all these people.

I am able to go to the yard and play sports, work out, and most of all get a suntan. You have no idea how good it feels to have the warm rays of the sun on your skin after being deprived of it for so many years. So I am getting some of my color back!

I have some very good news for you! Last week I got my first contact visit in thirteen years. It was pretty amazing! My family and a girl I know came to see me. It was so cool to be able to hug and kiss my loved ones after all these years. It was surreal. I never thought it could be possible. If you had told me 31 months ago that this was going to happen, I'd have thought it was crazy talk. Yet it happened and it was amazing. I had the biggest smile ever!

Marty with his friend Rubi, first contact visit in 13 years .

An Old Friend

It's very rare to find someone in life you can call a true friend.

I believe in life we come across many acquaintances and out of those, there are a small select few we can call a true friend.

A friend to me is categorized as an individual who cares for another, gives advice, someone who does not judge, and most of all has a mutual respect for the other person.

Trust and loyalty go without saying, and develop over time and through shared experiences.

I have met many people from all walks of life both in and out of prison. And we all have our own perspective on what we consider a friend.

I have maybe had a handful of friends, and out of these I have maybe had one true friend. Call it fate or chance, but this person came into my life at the darkest moment and has been a beacon of light in my life.

This person has shown me kindness, compassion, understanding, respect, trust, encouragement, and restored my faith in humanity.

Who knows why our paths crossed, or why this person took a chance on me and took the time to look past my mistakes and get to know the real me. I have never been big on expressing my feelings, yet I feel a desire to let it be known that the love I have for this person is unconditional.

I admire, respect, love and am thankful for the bond and friendship I have with my friend Katya.

A Day By The Sea

There have been many days and weeks I have spent with the sounds and smells of the sea during my years growing up near the beach. And as I got older my work as a stone mason afforded me the opportunity to combine two things that I love.

A day by the sea can wash away the stresses of life by allowing one to enjoy what nature has provided for us. To dig your toes in the warm sand, or to soak up the sun, or to take a dip in the cold sea is an experience one will remember young or old.

These moments should be shared with loved ones so these memories are never forgotten. There may be a time in our life such memories are unable to be created. And we'll not be able to reflect on nor cherish those moments.

A day by the sea is a distant memory for me. Yet the bars and cold concrete walls cannot keep one from reminiscing on days past. The smells of the salty sea air are as fresh today as they were back then, all because I was able to spend a day by the sea.

My Hands

Weathered, large and strong. Cracked and calloused from a life of strife. They have been used to caress and to create works of art in stone and on paper with the desire that they stand the test of time and inspire others to use their hands.

My hands I use to create the words you read. They are unique because they are mine and the talents they possess are only a small fraction of their true potential.

My hands, to touch, to caress, to create, to embrace, to write, to draw, to shake, to hold. To love, to fight, to fix and to inspire.

H ello my dear friend

A rtist of excellence

P risoner in body but never in spirit

P oised to fly free again

Y ou deserve to be celebrated

B orn 38 years ago

I nnocent as any new soul

R eaching always to better yourself

T rying to manifest your god given talents

H opeful that you will triumph

D ay by day

A lways staying positive, despite great challenges

Y ay, I say yay, Marty, I am blessed to know you.

November 1, 2015

Katya, I just received your correspondence dated 1/16/16. It was good to hear from you. And of course you can use whatever you want of mine in your Prison Wisdom book. You have my permission. I trust you as well! Just send me a copy of what you write. That's good enough for me.

Marty's drawing of his grandmother, from
a small photo taken in 1931

One of Marty's "sexy" women (abridged version!)

Katya

A singing bird for my Archival Singing Bird Press logo

Marty's Tiger
323

Katya, a simple gesture of appreciation for our friendship.

love marty

When I opened the Tiger card, this is what Marty had written inside, in beautiful calligraphy

Another of Marty's birds...

Marcia Suttenberg

 I have known Marcia Suttenberg since my feminist days in Portland, Oregon, in the 1970s. We were part of a political community advocating for various causes: anti-war, anti-racism, pro-women's liberation. I left Oregon in 1978 to seek my fortune elsewhere, living in Virginia, Oklahoma, and finally, Florida, which has been my home for 25 years. In all this time, Marcia and I have stayed in touch.

I was shocked, as were all her friends and colleagues, when she had to serve time in prison (two years) for an altercation with her soon-to-be ex-husband. I was able to visit Oregon during her imprisonment and see her—wearing her blue uniform, just as vital and alive as ever, despite the challenges of being locked-up.

When she was released, she re-married, continued her work as a political activist and artist and welcomed her first grandchild.

Marcia is the only pen pal that I knew before she went to prison, and I'm sorry that I cannot put my hands on the correspondence we shared while she was behind bars. While I was preparing this book, I asked her if she would be willing to sum up her experience as an educated, middle class, professional woman who ended up serving time. How was it different and how was it the same for her, as it was for the women she met during her incarceration? Did her "privileged" background offer her any advantages? How did being in prison transform her? What were her lessons learned?

I am happy to include some of the sketches she made while imprisoned. As an artist, I believe recording her life as an inmate offered a certain consolation, much as I believe writing offers to those who find themselves incarcerated.

I share Marcia's reflections now.

Prison Reflections

During the 1990's, in my early 40s, I served two years in the state penitentiary for inappropriately fighting back against my now ex- husband. I entered prison feeling angry and victimized and confused and sort of hopeless. As a middle class educated professional I was not the typical inmate. But I discovered inside that the 'sisters in blue' were in many ways equally bonded by our incarceration. And it was strangely comforting to be judged in a community not by wealth, or having good clothes, or a house in the right neighborhood, or a successful husband, or brilliant children, or prestigious career. If you gave respect to others, it was usually returned.

To pass my time I signed up for every activity offered! Computer classes, community college literature classes, Richard Simmons exercise videos, (dancing to the oldies was a high point of my two years), Native American sweats, ceramics classes, and talk therapy circles. I got a job on the grounds crew and loved being locked in a razor wired topped field by myself cutting the grass, or laying gravel for a new running path. I learned to play cards (spades), and throw dice. My roommate, who was doing 25 years, spent a lot of time crocheting Barbie clothes for her grandchildren. Seeing how she managed her time quickly got me over my shock at having two years of my life taken from me.

My best friends were a black woman my age, educated, who had received a two year sentence for biting the hand of a police officer during a dispute over a taxi fare. She was charged with attempted murder because she was HIV positive. We often walked the track together talking about food and soft pillows.

My other close friend was a young white skinhead who I met one night in the laundry room. She was in for a gang related attack on an African man. It was her 21st birthday, and she was crying because she missed her baby daughter. She was tough. I was the first Jew she had ever met. She had really deep working class anger, but she was also so bright and full of a desire to change the world she lived in, even though sadly she chose the wrong people to blame. She dreamed of becoming a nurse. I can only hope that our many conversations about politics rubbed off a little when she got out.

In my literature class we read Madame Bovary and it was one of the best discussions I have ever had about a classic novel. People completely understood Emma's desire to escape poverty. They had different reactions to her feelings about being trapped by her boring pharmacist middle class husband. Most thought she was stupid to have trusted Rodolphe, and there was intense discussion about her subsequent suicide. It was such an authentic real kind of sharing. No intellectual pretensions.

I so appreciated all of those who came into the prison to share their skills and acknowledge the basic needs and humanness of the inmates. For many it was the first time they got to participate in sharing their ideas, or writing a poem, or speaking up without fear of feeling stupid or inadequate.

Sure there were times when the hours seemed interminable, when the guards seemed unfair, the food gross (we called it mystery meat), the rules petty, (you weren't allowed to share toothpaste or candy bars, or to hug someone who was crying, for instance), and the strip searches after visits with our family so demeaning. But we developed special bonds and learned to see our similarities and appreciate each other – despite the fights that also so easily erupted. One night around the holidays we were allowed to have music and dance. There was one woman, in her 70's, who was doing a long sentence for shooting a sheriff – we made a big circle around her and all sang the Bob Marley song with love and gusto.

I left prison grateful for having a time out at a tough period in my life. I learned something about my internal rather than external self. So many stereotypes dissolved. I no longer feared loneliness. I learned to manage my anger. I learned to stand up for myself, yet also to know when to back off -- that sometimes my feelings or opinions didn't really matter at all. I admit I never really experienced remorse over my crime, but I accepted the consequences of my actions, and certainly learned to think before acting. In many ways I now hold it as a high point in my life.

2015

Reading on her bunk

On tiptoe to see out the window

Visiting through a pane of glass

The Troll and the Prince, a Fable

Dearest Katya, I was afraid I no longer had this story. I'm glad you typed it up for me or there would have been a good chance I would have tossed it out. I went through my legal locker and found it. Over the past five years or so I've downsized, getting rid of a lot of stuff that was written down, and so I'm just glad this wasn't one of them.

I hadn't read it in years, so I read it again and it's hard to believe this was written almost twenty-five years ago.

I remember it was after the Christmas party that some volunteers put together for us. Back then we were taken to the visiting park and there were candles on the table. A Quaker lady sat down and started talking to me, and she had the clearest eyes. Just looking into them was a blessing. And so later that night I sat down and was inspired to write this story.

My thanks to everyone who has clear eyes and an open heart.

David

The Troll And The Prince

Once upon a time there lived a boy. He was kind, cute and innocent. He lived in the land of giants. There was one giant who was very rough with him. It would tell him that he was ugly and that he was a bad boy and a monster. So, he started acting out that role. He grew up in the fashion of a troll. He would rob, steal and kill just to meet his needs. But oh, was he miserable, his inner pain was so haunting. Since he was only concerned with himself he could never see how beautiful life really was.

Then, on a Spring day he went down to a lake whose water was so clear and pure he was able to see a face in it. He screamed and hollered at it: "How dare you look upon me in the fashion that you do. Don't you know that I am the meanest and baddest troll around? With a face like yours I will surely destroy you, for you are weak."

The face in the water smiled and looked with eyes of compassion and said with a gentle voice: "I have known you for a long time, longer than you have known

333

your self. You have been taught the art of violence and it has brought you much pain as well as others. You have been deceived and you have acted as though your delusions were true. My friend they are not. You are good. You are beauty instead of destruction and darkness. You are a child of light and creativity."

The troll got mad and said "You son of a bitch! How dare you talk to me like that, for I am what I am." With a mighty force he kicked the face in the water causing huge waves to rise and the face disappeared.

The troll left and went and sat down under a tree and fell asleep. He started to dream of a little boy who was so loving and free spirited, so kind and giving, he knew no fear. He saw a giant beating on him and tears of pain in the little boy's eyes. Despite the beating the little boy was still so sweet. He saw the troll and walked up to him and hugged him, then vanished in the troll's arms.

The troll woke up feeling sad and confused. That dream seemed so real and for some reason he felt as though he knew that boy.

As the sun rose and birds began to chirp their morning love songs to life, the troll listened to them, and wondered why have I not listened to them before? (Or have I?)

He decided to go back to the lake, for he was very thirsty. He remembered the face he destroyed the day before. Now that brought a smile upon his face, but only for a second because when he reached the shore, there was the face with the eyes of compassion looking into his with much warmth.

The troll was really confused and said, "This cannot be for you are dead. How is it that I see you?"

This time the face did not say anything but let his eyes go deeper and deeper into the troll's eyes. All of a sudden the troll began to "see" his whole life from the beginning until the time of his death. The more he realized how false his life had been the clearer the face in the water and he realized that it was his own reflection. It was truly his face and it was beautiful, for a radiant light shone from it.

He heard an inner voice say, "My child, my child you have finally come home. I have been waiting for you all this time. You are no longer called a troll but a prince of light. You have known sadness, pain and suffering, hate and destruction. Now you will know the joy of giving yourself to life. Your radiance shall flow.

No longer will you hate others because you hate yourself. You will now share the blessings life has bestowed upon you. There is no longer a need to feel sorry for yourself, for you are truly strong."

The prince wept with joy for he knew that he was free. The troll died there at the lake of consciousness, and in its place the prince arose.

So if you ever go to a quiet lake and "see" the eyes of compassion don't be afraid for they are yours, your true self shining through waiting for you to come home.

David Dillbeck

EPILOGUE

When I taught my first class to inmates in 1991, I could never have imagined that, 25 years later, I would compile a book and call it *Prison Wisdom*. I only knew that I wanted to give copies to my students of their writing, so they could always remember what we had created and shared together.

In 2014, I was privileged to be invited to place my collected writings in an archive (at the University of Massachusetts, in Amherst). As I began to go through my manuscripts, I came across the prison anthologies I had put together, and it occurred to me that these words should not just sit on a shelf "waiting to be discovered" by a doctoral student in the future, or someone who was researching the criminal justice system of times past.

I flipped through the compiled pages, glancing at the poems and prose pieces, and I was so moved by what I read (how had I forgotten the poignancy of those words?), that I made up my mind then and there to put together a book—this book that you now hold in your hands.

I also had correspondence in my possession from many years of writing to prison pen pals. I wanted to honor those individuals—not only their letters, but the artwork they so generously shared with me. Thus, I envisioned including both the class writing and the pen pal material in *Prison Wisdom*.

It took me a long time to come up with a way of organizing the manuscript. I even hired a "coach" to help me persevere. Despite my best intentions, I became discouraged and put the idea on a shelf, saying I would "come back to it later." I used that time (a year, as it turned out) to create 14 compilations of my writing (primarily essays, poetry and fiction) to send a first shipment to the archive.

Once that was done, the Muse took me in hand and gave me new insight, or renewed energy, to continue. It was then, as I tackled the *Prison Wisdom* manuscript again, that I happened to attend a conference where, around a lunch table, I met Jeff Stoner. Turns out he ran a press that focused on publishing "works that inspire."

"I think I have one that fits that description," I told him.

The rest, as they say, is history. Once I knew I had a publisher, EWH Press, it was much easier to pursue my dream of sharing *Prison Wisdom* with the world, and I set my mind to it with renewed passion.

I was 47 years old when I entered Leon County Jail to offer my first ever class to inmates. Now 72, I look back over those years and all the individuals whose lives have touched mine, both students and pen pals, and I think, *So this then, is how it happens. One action can lead to another, and then to another, until one's life takes on meaning that one never could have imagined at the onset.*

I do not say lightly that this book is the result of my "prison ministry." And what is it to minister to another? It is to hold up a mirror—so a person may see their best self looking back, a human self that deserves to be valued, and yes, redeemed (for who amongst us does not want to be freed from the prisons that bind us?) And, truly, these individuals held up a mirror to me, as well.

I hope this book has inspired you and that the human stories you have read here have touched you. If so, I am satisfied that *Prison Wisdom* has done its perfect work.

As one of my students, Jewel, put it so well:

"When I tell a story, I want the reader to cry when I cried, laugh when I laughed. Ah yes, it is the telling of the story that fulfills my longing soul...."

Katya Sabaroff Taylor
Summer 2016

Acknowledgements

First I must acknowledge all the individuals who appear in this book, with gratitude for sharing your lives, stories and art with me.

Thanks to my publisher Jeff Stoner of EWH press and my graphic designer Bryan Mitchell for the meticulous care and devotion they gave to finalizing and upgrading the manuscript into its present form.

Thanks to my husband Tom for encouraging me when I needed it most and for affirming the value of this project from its inception.

Thanks to all the friends who listened to both my woes and joys and never lost faith that this book was meant to be.

Thanks to my readers for sharing *Prison Wisdom* with others who you think would benefit from its message.

Finally, thanks to those who work tirelessly to make prisons more humane, whether as paid staff or as volunteers. I have been fortunate to work with some very caring and enlightened individuals in my more than two decades offering writing classes to those behind bars.

CPSIA information can be obtained
at www.ICGtesting.com
Printed in the USA
FSOW03n0038290417
33560FS